Homer Laughlin China
An Identification Guide to Shapes & Patterns

Darlene Nossaman and Jo Cunningham

Schiffer Publishing Ltd

4880 Lower Valley Road, Atglen, PA 19310 USA

Dedications

This book is dedicated to the memory of two very special people in my life, Ann Kerr and Don Schreckengost. Ann was the dearest friend of my lifetime, my mentor, my encourager and confidante. Ann was not only a grand lady but was the country's leading authority of Russel Wright. Ann passed away in September of 2001. Don Schreckengost was a multi-talented gentleman, always willing to share his vast and remarkable knowledge of the American pottery industry with anyone seeking that information. My special friend "Schreck" passed away December 24, 2001. I will miss his friendship, the phone calls, the visits and his wonderful stories, which he always preceded by saying "This is very interesting" and they were. My life has been truly blessed by these two special friends and I will deeply miss Ann and "Schreck". My heart will never be the same.

Jo Cunningham

This book is dedicated to my husband, Norman, for his love and support. Also, in memory of my father who shared my interest in "old dishes."

Darlene Nossaman

Danube shape individual tea set.

Published by Schiffer Publishing Ltd.
4880 Lower Valley Road
Atglen, PA 19310
Phone: (610) 593-1777; Fax: (610) 593-2002
E-mail: Schifferbk@aol.com
Please visit our web site catalog at **www.schifferbooks.com**
We are always looking for people to write books on new and related subjects. If you have an idea for a book, please contact us at the above address.

Designed by "Sue"
Type set in Geometr 231Hv BT/Aldine721 BT
ISBN: 0-7643-1483-1
Printed in China
1 2 3 4

This book may be purchased from the publisher.
Include $3.95 for shipping. Please try your bookstore first.
You may write for a free catalog.

In Europe, Schiffer books are distributed by
Bushwood Books
6 Marksbury Ave. Kew Gardens
Surrey TW9 4JF England
Phone: 44 (0)20 8392-8585; Fax: 44 (0)20 8392-9876
E-mail: Bushwd@aol.com
Free postage in the UK. Europe: air mail at cost.
Please try your bookstore first.

Contents

How To Use This Book

This dinnerware identification guide has been written to be user friendly, for both beginning and advanced Homer Laughlin china collectors.

Knowing the shape of the ware is the most useful information that the collector can have in identifying their item. The dinnerware shapes are listed alphabetically in this guide. We hope that there will be enough information in your backstamp to easily guide you to the correct location for that shape.

Only Homer Laughlin China Company official names or decoration numbers are used in this guide. On a few occasions a temporary name has been added, to identify these decorations.

When you realize that there are nearly a hundred Homer Laughlin dinnerware *shapes* and possibly more than 12,000 *decorations*, you can understand why a particular decoration may not yet be identified. There are also many different pieces and sizes of the shapes that are not listed here. Collectors are welcome to send pictures of their items to the authors in care of the publisher as our research is on going. We would love to hear from you.

Acknowledgments

We wish to thank the many people who have offered assistance, pictures, and above all, encouragement with the undertaking of compiling and identifying as many shapes and patterns as possible of Homer Laughlin china. Collectors have generously offered time and assistance by sending pictures and identifications for this book. A special thank you to Mr. Marcus Aaron II, Mr. Joe Wells II, Mr. Joe Wells III, David Conley and staff at the Homer Laughlin China Company for their hospitality in allowing us to research old files.

We also wish to thank Mr. Don Schreckengost, Mr. Ed Carson Dennis Newbury and Mrs. Joe Wells III for answering endless questions and generously supplying information. Thanks also to Judi Noble and the art department staff for allowing us to invade their workspace and pointing out different areas in their department where important information might be lurking. Thanks also go to Laura Zeh and the capable staff at the Museum of Ceramics for always being willing to answer questions. And to all of our friends in the East Liverpool area please accept our thanks and know that we could not have accomplished this book without your help.

Special thanks go to Lori Fuller at the Radkow Library of the Corning Museum and Michael Duncan of the McLellan County Library for their willingness to help with this project. And thanks also to Dr. Margaret Carney, Director and Chief Curator at the Schein-Joseph International Museum of Ceramic Art and William C. Gates, Curator of History at the Ohio Historical Society, Gene and Barbara Andrews, Linda Cullin, Rockford and Robin

Estell, Stephanie and Brian Fischer, Miranda Goodby, Jerri Graves, Barbara Koehler, Sophia Papapanu, Pat Preuss, Becky Robbins, Roger Ronald Ruddy, Dr. Ralph Sheets, Mary Jo Stanton, Ed and Justine Vidrios, and special photographer Connie Hougardy.

We apologize if we have inadvertently left out any person or any organization who may have helped us make our dream of identifying Homer Laughlin China Company shapes and patterns a reality. Thanks to each one of you. Jo and Darlene

Photographs and/or pieces were provided by:
Mr. and Mrs. John Austin, Diane Baker, Kathleen Barnett, Marden and Marie Blackledge, Elaine Borowski, Shalene Blackwood, Cheryl Broderick, David Conley, Eb DeLong, Darrell Ertzberger, Candy Fagerlin, Gary Gieselman, Carla Grusz, Mark Gonzalez, Mary Gunderson, Terri and Randy Hjetland, Jack and Mary Ann Johnston, Barbara Koehler, Allen Kleinbeck, Bill Mackall, Fred Morse, John Moses, Fred Mutchler, Carl Moore Jr., Ed Pailer, Ralph Palmieri, Seth Price, Michael Rechel, Jo Rice, Don and Carolyn Riffel, Alyn Rosa, Steve Sfakis, Cynthia Stewart, Billy Stratton, Terry Telford, George Vincel, Ray Vlach, Matthew Whalen, Judi Wilfong and Joan Witt.

And to Jo's favorite photographers, Miss Crystal and Mr. Leland, thanks for taking great pictures, wonderful conversations, Mr. Leland's meticulousness, and Miss Crystal's patience during that meticulousness when she was asked to "move that piece to the left just a tiny bit." The results have been worth it all.

Introduction

This *Homer Laughlin China Guide to Shapes & Patterns* is designed to help collectors identify shapes, decorations, and patterns of the dinnerware made by The Homer Laughlin China Company. Our goal has been to provide the information as accurately as possible. We have researched old files at the company, looked through trade journals, publications and old catalogs. We have studied the backstamp information available. The information provided in this identification guide represents thirty-plus years of combined dinnerware research on the part of the authors. This identification guide has truly been a labor of love for both of us. Our hope is that readers and collectors will benefit from our efforts.

Shapes

The shape of the dinnerware is the most important key to its identification. Collectors should pay particular attention to the different shapes of dinnerware. Potteries named the shapes of their ware, which not only helped buyers distinguish which ware to order, but it also provided the potteries an opportunity to develop new shapes to offer their customers. The Homer Laughlin China Company continually developed shapes throughout the year, which allowed them to offer new shapes at the trade shows. In most instances, modelers and designers would be working on two or three different shapes at the same time.

The practice of mixing shapes within a set was a common practice with pottery companies and Homer Laughlin Company was no exception. The mixing of shapes within the set provided the pottery an opportunity to offer "something new and fresh" to their customers. While it may have been good business for the potteries it certainly causes confusion to the dinnerware collectors and researchers. We have included some of the "mixed-sets" with the hope of clearing up some of the same pattern-different shapes confusion.

Another confusing and puzzling question arises when collectors find different dates in the backstamp on their set or partial set of dinnerware. A former pottery employee offered the following explanation. "Different pieces for each shape were stored in a different room, such as cups in one room, bowls in another, etc. When orders were to be filled, this undecorated ware was pulled from the shelves. Some pieces might have been on the shelves longer than the other pieces, but little attention was paid to which pieces were pulled, thus the different dates."

There are many miscellaneous pieces that do not seem to fit into any section of this book. In the 1920s, a cup was advertised as the Oak shape (see page 168), while yet another sales sheet from company records shows many different shapes of cups made by The Homer Laughlin China Company.

Jubilee shape coffee server marked Debutante (same shape as Jubilee), mixed shape set, Gardenia decoration for Woolworth's.

GARDENIA PATTERN W-150

16 PIECE STARTER SET

PLATE 8" PLATE 7" PLATE 6" PLATE 5" PLATE 4" TEA CUP DISH 10"

BOWL 36 COV'D. TEAPOT FRUIT 4" TEA SAUCER

SAUCEBOAT OATMEAL 36 CREAM DISH 8"

DEEP PLATE 6" COV'D SUGAR

DOUBLE EGG CUP JUBILEE COFFE POT NAPPY 7" BAKER 7" PICKLE

W-150 Scheme Naut. Ivory "Gardenia"

GARDENIA PATTERN — OPEN STOCK

The Homer Laughlin China Co.

NEWELL, WEST VIRGINIA

Opposite page:
Mixed shapes (Nautilus Eggshell, Nautilus Regular, Jubilee),
Gardenia decoration number W150.

Decorations

Records indicate that the Homer Laughlin Company may have applied more than 12,000 decorations to their dinnerware. This seems to be an enormous number of decorations, but when you consider that the company's first ware came out of the kiln in October 1874, and that the company has been called "the largest manufacturer of American dinnerware", then that number becomes more realistic. While shapes were given names, decorations or decalcomanias were given a number or a name, or name and numbers. In most cases the first letter indicated the shape on which the decoration name or number was applied. Many times the same decalcomania was applied to several different shapes and given a new and different name. On some occasions the name remained the same. The name of the decoration would change when the same set was sold to different companies. Also, the name and the number of the decoration were also subject to change when even a sprig or decorative line was added. During the early part of the 1900s gold letters and numbers were a means of identification and were applied on the bottom of platters, plates and bowls but they are more often found under the lids of casseroles. These gold decoration numbers are important information to dinnerware researchers.

Decorations were applied to the ware by gold stamps, transfers and decalcomanias. Some of the early decal companies were Myercord, Palm Brothers, C. W. Harrison, Croxall, Ceramic T Company, Palm Fechteler and Speakman. The largest supplier of decalcomanias was the Rudolph Gaertner Company.

Two different preparations of gold were used to either line or to gold stamp decorations. One was a commercial solution called "liquid bright gold" and the other was a simple but very expensive gold bullion that was melted down with acids to the right consistency for the matte gold. These early pieces were marked with a B (bright) or an M (matte) denoting which gold was used on the item.

Trade Measurements

Standard measurements were a carry over from the old English way of conducting pottery business. The Homer Laughlin China Company used these trade measurements until the late 1950s. Trade measurements are not actual measurements of the ware. Both trade measurements and actual measurements are used in this book depending on the resource we were using. We have included information on the old trade measurements so the collector will be able to convert the measurements to actual sizes. The following information is from a 1926 Homer Laughlin catalog:

"The utmost care should be used in ordering. Pottery of catalog names and sizes, not actual sizes should always be specified. Pottery sizes vary considerably from actual sizes. This is not as it should be, but is an old custom followed in Europe and America and cannot readily be changed.

"Shown in parallel columns are the trade names of the principal articles in a china line. The trade names should always be used in ordering, as the common names are too indefinite and are sure to lead to confusion."

Actual sizes of pieces as listed in a 1920s wholesale catalog

Trade Name	Actual Size	Common Name
Plate 4"	6"	Bread & Butter
Plate 5"	7"	Pie plate
Plate 6"	8"	Breakfast plate
Plate 7"	8 3/4"	Dinner plate
Plate 8"	9 3/4"	Large dinner plate
Coupe soup 7"	8"	Soup plate with rim
Soup plate 7"	8 3/4"	Soup plate with rim
Baker 7"	6 1/2" x 8 3/4"	Oval vegetable dish
Covered dish	5 1/4" x 7 3/4"	Oval vegetable dish covered
Casserole 7"	5 1/4" x 7 3/4"	Round vegetable dish covered
Dish 8"	7 1/4" x 11 1/4"	Oval meat dish/platter
Dish 10"	8 3/4" x 15"	Oval meat platter
Dish 12"	10" x 15"	Oval meat dish/platter
Fruit 4"	5 1/8"	Sauce dish/dessert dish

Tea cups were listed in the wholesale catalog and measurements were 3 1/2" x 2".
Coffee cups were 3 3/4" x 2 1/2"
Saucers for coffee cups were listed as 6" while tea saucers were 5 1/2"
Fruit saucers or individual round dishes are trade size 4", actual size 5 1/8". Oatmeal bowls were listed as 6" actual size
Jugs were measured in height and capacity and were commonly called pitchers
Sauceboats were measured in height and capacity and were commonly called gravy boats, this confusing method of measurements was phased out in the late 1950s.

Sizing

We have been told that the numbering system had to do with how many pieces could be packed in a cask or packing barrel. We now know that this is a very old measuring system that dates back to England in the 1700s and has nothing to do with packing. Sizes of jugs or pitchers in the old catalogs were indicated by numbers such as 2s, 4s, 6s, 12s, 24s, 30s, 36s, 42s and 48s. The larger the number the smaller the piece and the smaller the number the larger the piece. Sugars were also listed in three sizes. This is yet another of the old English systems that carried over into the American Pottery Industry. I am indebted to Miranda Goodby, Senior Museum Officer-Ceramics of The Stoke-on-Trent Potteries Museum and Art Gallery for her help with this information.

While the early potteries priced their ware by the dozen, it wasn't necessarily an actual count of twelve. A unit of size was adopted and the size of the piece determined the number constituting a dozen. From a book *Relief-Moulded Jugs 1820-1890*, Antique Collectors Club, 1984, by R.K. Wood, we find that "all items of hollow-ware, of whatever shape, containing one pint are counted as 12 to the dozen. If they contain less, the quantity is increased; if they contain more the quantity is diminished. e.g. a 6-pint vessel would be 2 to the dozen. Prices were quoted per dozen." It seems safe to say that the larger the piece, the smaller the count of "the dozen." There were also variations in these sizes in early days of the pottery industry, depending upon the potter who made the piece.

Jugs:	Sugar bowls:
2s	30s
4s	36s
6s	24s
12s	
24s	
30s	
36s	
42s	

Marking System and Backstamps

1874 The words Porcelain Granite arched above a coat of arms with Laughlin Bros. in block letters below.

1876-1904 Two variations of the American Eagle astride the prostrate British Lion signifying the end of the domination of the British in the dinnerware field in this country was used. The early ware was marked "premium stone china". Also during this time period, Homer Laughlin in block letters with the L underlining Laughlin was used.

1886-1889 Horseshoe crossed swords with the lettering Laughlin China

1900-1909 Same Homer Laughlin in block letters followed by numbers. The first number designated the month from 1 to 12. The second single number indicated the year, and the last number 1, 2, or 3 designated the three East Liverpool, Ohio plants.

After 1900 the Homer Laughlin mark was used with variations from 1900 to 1960. Some marks will have the shape name, some only the date, "Hotel ware" or "Made in USA" under the HLC backstamp.

1910-1919 Same Homer Laughlin in block letters, followed by a letter which was used to designate the month, with one or two digit numbers indicating the year and the plant was indicated by the letter L for Laughlin East End plant, 4 was "N", and N5 was plant number 5.

1920-1929 Same Homer Laughlin in block letters, followed by a number which was used to designate the month, one or two digit numbers for the year and letter and number for the plant.

1930-1969 Same Homer Laughlin in block letters. The month was expressed as a letter, and the year was indicated with two numbers. Plant No. 4 was "N", No. 5 was "R". Nos. 6 and 7 were "C" and No. 8 was listed as "P", but in most instances, only N and the plant number appear on the backstamps.

1970-1980 Only the Homer Laughlin name and a year of manufacture appear.

1981 Hollowware items were marked with a raised logo of the Homer Laughlin trademark.

Backstamp Information
From a 1912 Homer Laughlin China Company catalog:

This trade-mark name on the underside of a dish is our guarantee to merchant and consumer that the piece bearing it is of high quality, honestly made, and "as good as it looks." *The Homer Laughlin China Co.*

In some cases distributors, such as Cunningham and Pickett, applied their own backstamp along with the HLC backstamp and along with the Cunningham and Pickett pattern name. At one point in their business relationship, Cunningham and Pickett requested that only their backstamp appear on the piece.

Many potteries purchased undecorated ware from the Homer Laughlin China Company. They would then add their own decorations or add an overlay of gold to existing patterns. You may find these pieces double stamped with both of the company names or just one of the names. Some of the *decorating companies* were:

Atlas China Company
Bromley
Eastern China
Kass China
Monarch Dinnerware Co.
Pacific China
Royal China
Stetson China Company

The Pearl China Company was a distributor whose ware was decorated at the Pioneer Pottery in East Liverpool, Ohio, and distributed under the Pearl China backstamp.

Backstamps

The following is a sample listing of *backstamps* which offer some clues as to the identification of the shape, design or for whom the piece was made. This list is far from complete, but some of the backstamps collectors will encounter are:

Old Sport Scenes
Famous Old Ships
Early American Homes
Americana scenes from Currier and Ives
American Subjects from Currier and Ives
Shakespeare Country
American China
Color Harmony
Tudor Rose for Quaker Oats
Kenmark China
Sunrise brand for Sears
Zylco
Royal Crown - AA1 Dinnerware
Palette Ware
Colorama

Brief History of the Homer Laughlin China

The Homer Laughlin China Company began as a two-kiln pottery along the banks of the Ohio River in East Liverpool, Ohio. Ground was broke for the new pottery in the fall of 1873 but it would be October 1874 before the first ware would be produced at the Ohio Valley Pottery Company. Homer and his brother Shakespeare were the original owners, but Shakespeare withdrew in 1877. The pottery continued under the name of Ohio Valley Pottery, Homer Laughlin, proprietor until 1896 when the pottery was incorporated under the name of The Homer Laughlin China Company.

From the beginning, only the most skilled workmen were employed and the demand for the Laughlin ware kept the pottery in almost continuous operation. During this time period the American potters were struggling to establish a name for their potteries against foreign imports. Only English pottery was desired by the American consumer and even the Sears catalogs touted American made pottery as inferior to English made ware. Homer Laughlin refused to give in to deceiving the public by using an English-looking backstamp and developed his Eagle over the Lion backstamp. In 1897 Mr. Laughlin sold his interest in the pottery to Mr. Louis I. Aaron and his sons, Charles and Marcus and Mr. W.E. Wells. Mr. Wells had been the bookkeeper for Mr. Laughlin since 1889 and would be one of the staying powers in the company until his retirement in 1930.

In 1905 the pottery began to move their operations across the Ohio River to the newly established town of Newell, West Virginia where it is still producing pottery under the capable leadership of the Aaron and Wells families. In 1929 all production at the East Liverpool plants ceased and the large Newell facility was the sole producer of Homer Laughlin China.

The following is a quote from an early 1900s Pittsburgh Dispatch newspaper. "The Homer Laughlin Company continues to make semi-porcelain ware of the highest order, while the decorations are in keeping with the body. Never for a moment has the reputation of the company been permitted to suffer because of the increase in output, and the same high standard attained in the old four kiln pottery in East Liverpool is maintained by the new corporation". This statement holds true for the present Homer Laughlin China Company operations and wares.

Names of Dinnerware Pieces

In December of 1965, the following memo was sent to the Homer Laughlin China Company department heads concerning the change in nomenclature of their dinnerware items:

Old Name	New Name
Tea cup	Cup
Tea saucer	Saucer
Plate 8"	Dinner 10"
Plate 7"	Luncheon 9"
Plate 6"	Salad 8"
Plate 5"	Salad 7"
Plate 4"	Bread and butter
Oatmeal 36s	Oatmeal
Lug soup	Lug soup
Chowder	Chowder soup
Plate 5"cereal soup	Cereal soup
Coupe 6"	Coupe soup 8"
Deep plate 6"	Rim soup
Dish 8"	Platter 11"
Dish 10"	Platter 13"
Chop plate	Platter round 13"
Nappy 7"	Vegetable
Baker 7"	Vegetable oval
Sauceboat	Sauceboat
Pickle dish	Sauceboat stand
Sugar covered	Sugar covered
Cream	Cream
Casserole covered	Casserole covered
Coffee server covered	Coffee pot covered
Covered butter	Covered butter
Salt	Salt
Pepper	Pepper
Ashtray	Ash tray
Square salad 6"	Square salad 6"
Coffee break cup	Coffee break cup

In 1972, a memo from Mr. J.M. Wells directed that the term "large soup" will identify coupe soups and rim soups. "Cereal soup" will identify lug soups, chowders and cereal soups.

Alphabetical Listing

Add+A+Place 1940

Add+A+Place is not a shape, but a promotional plan introduced in the spring of 1940 to a limited number of stores on a trial basis. In July 1941, the Add+A+Place plan was opened "to every customer, and to every customer in every city."

This plan was advertised as a convenient method of building a dinner set, one place setting at a time. A place setting consisted of one teacup, one saucer, one sauce dish, one 9", one 7", and one 6" plate. Serving groups of covered sugar and cream, or vegetable bowl and 13" platter, or gravy boat and pickle dish were also offered. Add+A+Place was offered on Nautilus Eggshell, Georgian Eggshell and at least one pattern was offered on the Theme Eggshell shape. Other shapes and decorations may have been offered under this sales promotion plan.

The Add+A+Place decoration numbers are:
Pattern name unknown N-1634
Whitehall shown N-1580
Moselle G-3302
Cynthia G-3351
Regency G-3357
Cordova G-3370
Pattern name unknown G-3388
Floral TH-5 (Theme shape)

Above right:
Eggshell Nautilus shape plate, Whitehall decoration for the Add+A+Place line. $8-10

Right:
Add+A+Place brochure showing Whitehall on the Eggshell Nautilus shape, decoration number N-1580

**BUILD YOUR DINNER SET
THE ADD+A+PLACE WAY**

6 PIECE SERVICE FOR ONE $1.00

One dinner plate 9", one salad plate 7", one bread and butter plate 6", one tea cup, one tea saucer, one sauce dish.

The above 6 pieces are available with larger dinner plate (10-inch) and lug-handled soup instead of 9-inch dinner plate and sauce dish........ $1.20

Make your dinner service as large as you wish—buy as many place-settings as you like for $1.00 a place! Select and organize your dinner set this modern and economical way.

Add-A-Place serving groups:
Covered sugar and cream......................$1.00
Vegetable bowl and platter 13".............1.00
Gravy boat and pickle dish.................1.00

Add-A-Place is the newest and smartest way to buy fine dinnerware economically. Buy exactly the number of places you need for your table. You do not get unnecessary and useless items.

Two different Add-A-Place settings are available—one six-piece place-service with 9-inch dinner plate and sauce dish; the other with large dinner plate (10-inch) and lug-handled soup.

Take advantage of this convenient method of building a dinner set tailored to fit your requirements. When you have this pattern, you can "Add a Place" at any time. Complete open stock is available at very reasonable prices.

Alliance 1960

The Alliance shape was designed in 1960 for the Alliance China Company of Alliance, Ohio, a subsidiary of the Cunningham and Pickett Company of Alliance, Ohio.

The Alliance shape was made up of the following pieces: **trade measurements** (see page 7 for an explanation of the old trade measurements):
Ash tray fluted 5 3/4"
Teacup
Teapot
Tea saucer
Sauceboat
Casserole/cover
Cream
Sugar/cover
Plates 8", 7", 5", 4" plates
Bowl coupe 6"
Bowl fruit 4"
Bowl 36s
Nappy 7"
Dish(platter) 8"
Dish (platter) 10"
Teapot/cover
Salt and Pepper, Cavalier shape

Alliance shape, Avalon decoration made for Cunningham and Pickett. Left to right front:
cup/saucer set $8-10
salt and pepper set $8-10
creamer $6-8
back row: plate $6-8
platter $12-15

Alliance shape, Linden decoration made for Cunningham and Pickett. Plate $6-8
cup/saucer set $8-10
cereal/fruit bowl $4-6

Amberstone 1967

The Amberstone Fiesta line was introduced in 1967 and has a rich brown glaze. The Amberstone flatware has a dark brown design, while the hollowware is a solid color. It was produced by The Homer Laughlin China Company and advertised as Sheffield dinnerware for supermarket continuity programs.

The Sheffield Amberstone was ordered directly from Sheffield Dinnerware, Customer Service Department, Newell, West Virginia.

Known Amberstone pieces made for Sheffield Dinnerware: **actual measurements**

Plate dinner 10"	Casserole covered
Dessert dish	Sauce boat
Plate bread and butter	Relish tray 13" metal handle
Coffee cup/saucer	Coffee server
Vegetable bowl	Tea server
Sugar covered	Butter dish covered
Creamer	Serving platter round 13"
Platter oval 13"	Salad bowl jumbo
Plate large soup	Jam jar covered
Ashtray	Mustard jar covered
Salt and pepper shakers	Pitcher serving
Plate salad 7"	Mug jumbo
Soup/cereal bowl	Plate pie

Items listed are from a 1970 Sheffield Amberstone dinnerware order blank. Fiesta shapes that were redesigned for the Amberstone line were teapot cover and knob, cereal/soup, creamer handle, casserole knob, pickle dish, 7" nappy, salad bowl, cup handle and the coffee pot knob.

Americana 1940s

Americana is the name given to this very collectible mixed shapes set. Americana was composed of the Willow, Brittany, Americana and Empress shapes. The only Americana shapes are the teapot, cover and the A.D. cups and saucers. The Americana line was an exclusive Montgomery Wards pink underglaze decoration and was number W-2553. It is marked "An American Subject, Currier and Ives Print, James Parr Engraver, Made in U.S.A. by Homer Laughlin" (all within a scrolled drawing)

Known Americana Currier and Ives decoration: trade measurements
Americana shapes:
Tea pot 36 oz.
Tea pot cover (the tea pot cover has a Willow knob)
A.D. cup and saucer

Willow Shapes:	Dish pickle 6"
Tea cups	Dish (platters) 8",10"12"
Cream	
Sugar (Willow lid)	**Empress:**
Sauceboat	Bowl fruit 4"
	Bowl coupe soup 7"
Brittany Shapes:	Baker 7"
Nappy covered 8"	Nappy 7"
Plates 4",5",7",8'	Tea Saucer

Left to right, Amberstone dinner plate $6-8
disc pitcher $55-60
saucer $2-4
cup $4-6

Amberstone pie baker $30-35
stick butter dish $40-45
covered casserole $50-55

Back row left to right: Amberstone salad plate
$2-4
soup bowl $12-14
front row: cereal/soup $5-7
cream $8-10
ash tray $30-35

Coffee, teapot and saucer were the only
Americana shape pieces in the Americana line. Americana A.D. coffee cup
$30-35

Americana shape teapot and cover
$125-135

American Beauty 1898

The American Beauty shape was advertised as a new design in 1898. The shape was described as beautiful, ornate and artistic design. The semi-porcelain quality is not to be equaled by any other American potter and superior to English pottery. It was available in undecorated glossy white, gold stamp and decorated patterns.

Shown is the Wood Violet decoration on American Beauty. It is described as a spray of purple wood violets, red and brown nasturtiums, with green leaves, gold stippled semi-porcelain. A 56-piece set of Wood Violet sold for $6.95 in the 1908 Sears catalog.

American Beauty pieces
shown from a 1901 Homer Laughlin catalog

Row 1: Item 1 sauce boat, Item 2 toast rack, Item 3 egg cup, Item 4 sugar, Item 5 teapot, Item 6 cream, Item 7 custard, Item 8 spooner, Item 9 jug

Row 2: Item 10 A.D. coffee and saucer, Item 11 teacup and saucer, Item 12 coffee cup and saucer, Item 13 pickle, Item 14 celery tray, Item 15 olive dish, Item 16 fruit dish, Item 17 individual butter, Item 18 bone dish,

Row 3: Item 19 covered butter, Item 20 bowl, Item 21 oyster bowl, Item 22 oatmeal bowl, Item 23 comportier, Item 24 coupe soup, Item 25 nappy, Item 26 baker

Row 4: Item 27 covered dish, Item 28 chop plate, Item 29 7" plate, Item 30 cake plate, Item 31 deep plate 7", Item 32 dish (platter)

Row 5: Item 33 oyster tureen, Item 34 casserole, Item 35 sauce tureen complete, Item 36 fruit bowl, Item 37 soup tureen complete.

American Beauty dinnerware shapes from an early Homer Laughlin catalog.

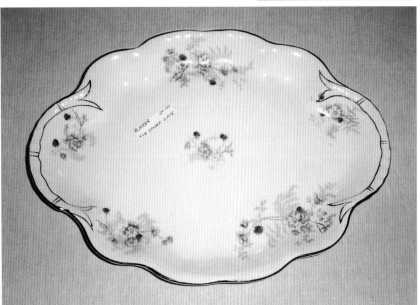

American Beauty shape platter, decoration number 414. $25-30

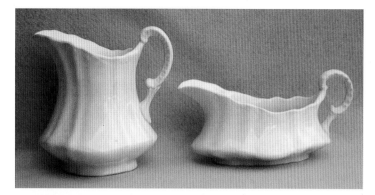

American Beauty shape, Glossy White decoration. pitcher $45-50
sauceboat $20-25

American Beauty shape olive dishes, Glossy White decoration. $20-25 each

American Beauty shape casserole, P-43 decoration. $35-40

American Beauty shape comport, decoration number 9953. $55-75

American Beauty shape celery tray, Pansy decoration. $50-60

American Beauty shape fruit bowl, Primrose Clusters decoration. $70-95

American Beauty shape teapot, Petite Alpine Rose decoration. $60-75

American Beauty shape cake plate, Trinity Roses decoration. $45-50

American Beauty shape spooner, Carnation decoration. $50-60

American Beauty shape casserole and cover, decoration number 331. $50-75

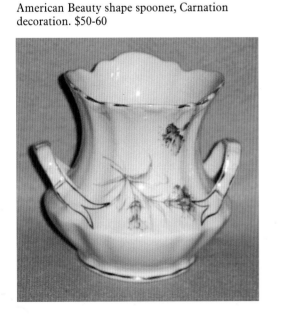

American China 1963

The American shape is another shape that we know very little about. The mold book for 1963 mentions the following pieces:
Cup
Saucer
Nappy 6"
Bowl cereal/soup
Coffee server

American China shape sugar and cream, Glossy White decoration. $20-25 set

American Traditional 1960s

There is very little information available on this shape. A 1963 catalog lists the following items in American Traditional: **trade measurements**

American Traditional shape, white undecorated cup $8-10 sugar and cover $12-14

Teacup/saucer
Plate 4"
Plate 8"
Cream
Sugar/cover
Bowl salad
Plate deep
Nappy covered
Plate square
Baker
Sauceboat
Pickle dish

American Vogue

see Vogue Mercantile

Anchor 1878

The Anchor shape is back-stamped "Shakespeare Laughlin, patent applied for August 1878 Premium Stone China". Shown is a picture of a small Anchor jug taken at the Museum of Ceramics, East Liverpool, Ohio.

Anchor shape jug, white undecorated. $150-175

Andover 1940

The Andover shape was designed for the Carson, Pirie and Scott Company to be used with their Carson Wishmaker series which combined different household goods into one ensemble for sale. The Andover shape is hollow ware only and was used in combination with the Swing shape flatware. Andover appears to not have many decorations, the most common is the Gordon decoration and is marked A-1.

Known items that made up the Andover line: **trade measurements**
Bowl 36s
Eggcup double

Andover shape:
Baker 7", 8"
Cream
Nappies 7", 8"
Bowl cream soup and stand
Bowl onion soup
Sauceboat fast stand

Sugar
Tea cup
Teapot

Swing shape:
Dish (platters)8", 10", 12"
Plates 4", 6", 8"
Saucer
Celery tray

Unknown shapes:
Bowls fruit, oatmeal
A.D. cup and saucer

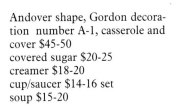

Andover shape, Gordon decoration number A-1, casserole and cover $45-50
covered sugar $20-25
creamer $18-20
cup/saucer $14-16 set
soup $15-20

The Angelus early 1900s

The Angelus is another early 1900s shape and is easily distinguished by the shape of the handles. Many sizes of pieces were made other than those listed. The Angelus was produced in both undecorated pure white and white with decorations.

Row 1: Item 1 teapot, Item 2 sugar and cover, Item 3 cream, Item 4 sauce boat, Item 5 covered butter, Item 6 bowl, Item 7 coffee cup and saucer, Item 8 tea cup and saucer, Item 9 A.D. cup and saucer
Row 2: Item 10 salad, Item 11 nappy, Item 12 baker, Item 13 oatmeal bowl, Item 14 fruit bowl, Item 15 individual butter, Item 16 bone dish, Item 17 spooner
Row 3: Item 18 dish (platter) Item 19 cake plate, Item 20 plate, Item 21 deep plate, Item 22 coupe soup, Item 23 pickle
Row 4: Item 24 oyster tureen, Item 25 casserole, Item 26 covered dish, Item 27 sauce tureen complete, Item 28 jug

Angelus shapes from an early Homer Laughlin catalog.

Angelus shape casserole and cover, "Vining Violets" decoration number 6015. $75-95

Angelus shape plate, Flow Blue decoration number 9983. $35-45

Angelus shape plate, Flowers and Ribbon decoration number W6S. $15-18

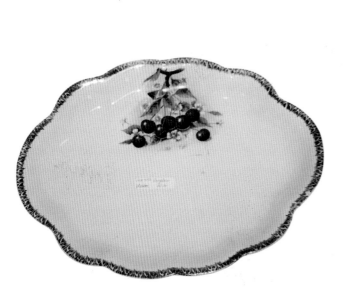

Angelus shape platter, Knox Cherries decoration number S41. $35-40

Angelus shape plate, Twin Flowers decoration number W8S. $15-18

Angelus shape plate, decoration number 487. $15-18

Angelus shape bone dish, decoration number 4919. $15-18

Angelus shape plate, Gold Stamp
decoration number 9952. $15-18

Angelus shape casserole lid, decoration number 9954. $15-20

Angelus shape pitcher, decoration number 4570.
$40-45

Angelus shape casserole and cover, Poppy decoration number 9994. $75-100

Angelus shape jugs, left H-60 decoration, right F.E.F. decoration. $35-40 each

Angelus shape, Princess decoration SR-275 for Sears Roebuck. butter dish and cover $95-100
butter pat, $6-8

Angelus shape covered casserole, decoration number 707. $50-75

Angelus shape sauceboat/gravy, white undecorated. $15-20

Angelus shape platter, Three Roses decoration number R-749. $25-30

Appletree Shape 1933

The Appletree set of five nesting bowls 5", 6", 7", 8", 9" was designed by Frederick Rhead. The Appletree bowls have embossed elongated trees, a style Mr. Rhead commonly used in his art pottery. The bowls are sometimes referred to as "Orange Tree Bowls". The bowls can be found undecorated in green, melon yellow, old ivory and turquoise with the most common color being turquoise. Japanese potters copied the Appletree bowls in 1936. Most of the Homer Laughlin Appletree bowls are incised HLC in the base. The same decorations that were used on OvenServe were also used on the Appletree bowls. There may be six sizes of Appletree bowls instead of the five listed in company records.

**Known decorations used on
the Appletree shape bowls:**

OS-50 Red edge
OS-51 Green edge
OS-54 Silver edge
OS-56 Blue edge
OS-63 3 Red lines
OS-64 3 Green lines
OS-65 2 sprigs (VR-232) silver edge line
OS-66 2 sprigs (VR-235) silver edge line
OS-86 3 sprigs (VR-128) silver edge line
OS-111 3 sprigs (747) silver edge line
OS-124 3 black lines
OS-134 3 blue lines

Appletree shape bowls, decoration number OS-62. The Appletree bowls have the OvenServe decoration numbers. larger bowl $70-75
hard to find smaller bowls expect to pay twice as much

Appletree shape bowl, decoration number OS-66. $70-75

Incised HLC mark used on Appletree shape bowls.

Appletree shape, six sizes of Turquoise bowls. Turquoise is the most common color found in the Appletree bowls. $260-280

Left: Appletree shape bowls, three green lines $70-75 each
Decoration number OS-64 top right, silver edge OS-54 $70-75
lower right three red lines OS-63 $275-300 set

Applique 1953

Applique is not a shape, but a process of decoration. The Applique process was a joint effort of The Homer Laughlin China Company and the E.I. DuPont de Nemour Company. Developed in 1953 the Applique process was "developed to give overglaze decorations of bold relief and colors, which were bright and resistant to both food acids and washing detergents." The Applique line was made up of the Brittany, Rhythm and Charm House shapes. Some solid color hollowware (Charm House and Rhythm) was used with the Applique line. The Charm House colored glaze colors were black, brown, chartreuse, dark green, yellow, and bright blue.

Brittany Flatware-actual measurements:
Tea saucer
Plate 10"
Plate 9"
Plate 7 1/4"
Plate 6 1/4"
Plate 5"
Plate 4"
Plate 8 1/4" deep plate (rim soup)
Bowl fruit 5 3/4"
Bowl oatmeal 6 1/4"
Nappy 9"
Dish 15" platter
Dish 13 1/2" platter

Rhythm Shape:
Pickle 9"
Sauceboat

Charm House Shape:
Tea cup
Sugar covered
Casserole covered
Cereal/ soup
Salt & pepper
Tea pot covered

Some of the decorations used on the Applique line include:
A-100 Yellow Daisy - Chain of yellow daisies and thin green leaves around rim.
A-101 Cherry Valley-Chain of cherries around the rim
A-102 Pennsylvania Dutch-Produced for J.J. Newberry stores and Colgate. The Pennsylvania Dutch decoration has red flowers; dark green and chartreuse leaves form wreath around the rim.
A-103 Black Eyed Susan-Made for F.W. Woolworth stores. The Black Eyed Susan decoration has yellow daisies, dark centers, and green leaves around the rim.
A-104 Apple-Made for the McCrory stores. Apple has red apples with green leaves around the rim.
A-105 Plaid-Made for Sears. The Plaid decoration is different combinations of blue, green, black and yellow plaids around the rim.

A-106 Tulip-Made for the G.G. Murphy stores in colors of red, yellow, chartreuse and greens

A-109 Sherbrooke also called Bayberry-Black, green, maroon and coral color combinations.

A-111 Spring Song-center decal of turquoise, yellows and gray

A-112 Mayfair-center decal in turquoise, gray, black and yellow

A-113 Pageant-diamond chain design

A-114 Star Tree-scattered snowflakes

A-115 Love Song (no picture)

Applique brochure showing the Yellow Daisy decoration.

Left: Applique line Brittany shape, Cherry Valley decoration number A-101, plate $10-12
right: Brittany shape sauceboat/liner, Pennsylvania Dutch decoration number A-102. A-102 was made for JJ Newberry and Colgates. $12-15

Left: Applique line Brittany shape plate, Plaid decoration number A-105 made for Sears. $10-12
right: Buttercup decoration $10-12

Applique line Brittany shape plate,
Orange Blossom decoration. $10-12

Applique line Brittany shape plate,
Strawberry decoration. $10-12

Applique line Charm House shape,
Yellow Daisy decoration number A-100.

Art China 1902

The Art China line is a line of decorated specialty items made by the Homer Laughlin China Company from about 1902 till about 1911. For a list of shapes and decoration names see *Homer Laughlin China, A Giant Among Dishes 1873 to 1939*, Jo Cunningham

Art China backstamp used on Homer Laughlin China Company's Decorated Specialties.

Barbara Jane

see Ivory Color

Bates, Lee 1958-1960

Lee Bates is a line of individual French casseroles with Indian style decorations produced in 1958-1960 for the Lee Bates Company of Albuquerque, New Mexico. Eight different decals were used on the Lee Bates individual casseroles. Lee Bates pieces are backstamped "Ovenproof, Detergent Proof © GU 30906 Lee Bates, Albuquerque, N.M. Made in America by American Craftsman in World's Largest Potteries."

Known Lee Bates French casseroles:
LB-1 Wagon Train in blue and black
LB-2 Square Dance in beige and black
LB-3 Round Up in red and black
LB-4 Buffalo Hunt in green and black
LB-5 (Indian on Horseback) Riders in blue and black
LB-6 Rodeo in beige and black
LB-7 Indian Dance in red and black
LB-8 Indian (Teepee)Village in green and black

Lee Bates backstamp

Lee Bates individual casseroles, left to right:, Indian Village, Riders, Indian Dance decoration. $12-15 each.

Best China 1960

Best China is The Homer Laughlin China Company's name for their food service lines. During the late 1950s, melamine and Japanese import dinnerware were stiff competition to the American potteries, so The Homer Laughlin Company decided to produce dinnerware for hotels, restaurants and other food institutions. Best China was introduced in 1960 as a fully vitrified china line. Plant No. 6 was adapted for this purpose and Carolyn was the first Best China shape produced.

Best China backstamp.

KIWI© BC-1346

Best China Carolyn shape, Kiwi decoration number BC-1346.

Big Pay Off

The Big Pay Off is not a shape name but a line sold to the Specialty China Company of Pittsburgh, Pennsylvania who then distributed the ware. Bess Myerson lent her name to the Big Pay Off premium line but did not actually design the decoration. The Big Pay Off decoration is on the Rhythm and Cavalier shapes and the decoration designation number is (Rhythm) RY-249. This decoration has also been found on other Homer Laughlin shapes.

Known Big Pay Off pieces: trade measurements
Tea cup
Tea saucer
Plate
Plate 8"
Plate 5"
Bowl coupe soup 7"
Fruit 4"
Nappy 7"
Dish (platter) 10"
Sugar covered Cavalier shape
Cream- Cavalier shape

Big Pay Off backstamp

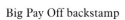

Rhythm shape, Big Pay Off - Bess Myerson line, cream $12-15 plate $10-12

Bristol 1970s

The Bristol shape was a short hollowware line consisting of cup, cream, sugar and cover. There may be other Bristol hollowware pieces.

Bristol shape hollowware.

Brittany 1936

The Brittany shape, introduced in 1936, was a re-working of the older Empress shape. It was redesigned in 1938 and again in the early 1970s when it was called Diplomat. Brittany was a long lived, popular shape and can be found with many different decorations. Brittany flatware was frequently used in mixed-shape sets and in the late 1950s was mixed with Cavalier but given the Brittany (B) designation.

Known pieces in the Brittany shape: trade measurements

Cup A.D.	Dish (platters) 8", 10"
Saucer A.D.	Egg cup double (Cable)
Bowl (Empress shape)	Bowl fruit 4"
Plate chop 10"	Bowl oatmeal 36s
Plate chop 8"	Nappies covered 7", 8"
Plates 6",7",8"	Sauceboat
Plate deep 6"	Sugar covered
Pickle dish 6"	Tea cup/ tea saucer
Cream	Teapot

Brittany shapes from Homer Laughlin China Company files.

Brittany shape, Green Ivy also called Ivy Chain decoration number B-1373. plate $10-12
cream $10-12
sugar $12-14

Brittany shape plate, Clive decoration number B-1316. $10-12

Brittany shape, Hemlock decoration number for maroon/red Hemlock B-2001.
cream $10-12
sugar $12-14

Right:
Brittany shape, green Hemlock decoration. plate $10-12

Below:
Brittany shape, Lily of the Valley decoration. cream $10-12, covered sugar $12-14

Brittany shape plate, Colonial variation decoration. $10-12

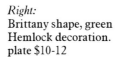

Brittany shape, Majestic decoration number W-538, also called
Lady Alice when sold to Wards in 1942 decoration number B-1317.
left to right: cream $10-12,
plate $10-12,
sugar and cover $12-14

Brittany shape plate, Promenade decoration number B-1438. $10-12

Brittany shape, Majestic W-538 from Homer
Laughlin China Company files.

Brittany shape small plate,
Rosewood decoration
number B-1315. Rosewood
was part of a combination
set made of Federal
glassware and Homer
Laughlin Rosewood
dinnerware marketed
under the Fairfield name.
$6-8

Brittany shape plate, yellow and blue Plaid decoration number
B-1203, rose and blue Plaid is decoration number B-1202, yellow
and black Plaid decoration number is B-1205. $10-12

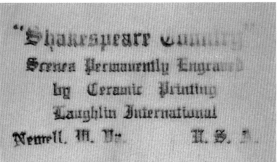

Brittany shape covered sugar, cream marked Royal Splendor, decoration number B-1346. $12-14

The Shakespeare Country line was made for Laughlin International on the Brittany shape. The creamer and sugar can be found with two different decoration styles.

Top: Later Brittany shape covered sugar and cream, Majestic/Lady Alice decoration. $20-25
Lower: Earlier Brittany shape covered sugar and cream, Shamrock decoration. $20-25

Backstamp on Brittany shape, Shakespeare Country decoration.

Brittany shape cup/saucer, Sylvan decoration number B-1399. $8-10

Front: Brittany shape, Shakespeare Country decoration. cup/saucer $10-12
sugar $10-12
cream $10-12
Back: plate $6-8
cereal bowl $4-6

Brittany shape, Shakespeare Country decoration, the center decoration on the plates are the same. The border decoration on the other pieces is different. The backstamp is the same. plate $10-12
covered sugar $12-14
cream $10-12
saucers $2-3 each

Brittany shape saucer, Stratford (yellow and gray), Stratford (pink and gray) decoration number B-1411. $2-3.

Brittany shape, decoration official name not known but aptly named by a collector as "String of Hearts." small plate $6-8 dinner plate $8-10 platter $15-18

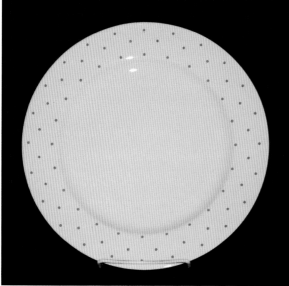

Brittany shape plate, "Blue Dots," also called Gaiety when sold to Wards in 1959. Sold with Studio shape hollowware. $8-10

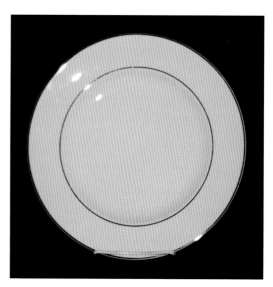

Brittany shape plate with platinum trim, decoration number B-1448. $8-10

CONSTELLATION PATTERN ★ ★   ★ ★

Sugar Pine . . . Another best selling pattern from the largest selection of moderately priced dinnerware. Smart . . . Sophisticated . . . in Pine Green and Cone Brown.

EASTERN SALES AND DISPLAY ROOM: SUITE 2000, 212 FIFTH AVE., NEW YORK 10, N. Y. . . . BERNARD MENGE
CHICAGO SALES OFFICE: ROOM 916, LA SALLE-WACKER BLDG., 221 NO. LA SALLE ST., CHICAGO 1, ILL. · N. W. MacDONALD

The Homer Laughlin China Co.
NEWELL   WEST VIRGINIA

Homer Laughlin China Company advertisement for the Brittany shape, Sugar Pine decoration number B-1437.

Cable Early 1900s

The Cable shape is an early ironstone ware produced around the turn of the century. Most all of the pottery companies produced the same or similar Cable shapes. While most of the pieces found are in the plain white ironstone ware some pieces were decorated. Shown are Cable and Sundry Toilet Wares from a 1914 Homer Laughlin catalog.

Cable and Sundry (miscellaneous) shapes from a 1920s Homer Laughlin China Company catalog.

THE HOMER LAUGHLIN CHINA COMPANY, NEWELL, W. VA.

CABLE AND SPECIAL ITEMS

1 W. W. Egg Cup	5 Baker, 7 inch, Cable	10 Plate, 7 inch, Cable	15 Ovide Tea	19 Mixing Bowl, 12s
2 Child's Mug	6 St. Denis Bowl, 30s	11 Dish, 10 inch, Cable	16 Octagon Covered Jug, 24s	20 Scalloped Nappy, 7 inch
3 Oyster Bowl, 30s, Cable	7 Celery Tray	12 Sauce Boat, Cable	17 Cable Mug, 30s	21 Fluted Nappy, 7 inch
4 Covered Butter, Cable	8 Fruit, 4 inch, Cable	13 Double Egg Cup	18 Oak Tea	22 Cable Jug, 24s
	9 Sugar, 30s, Cable	14 St. Denis Tea		

Page Seventeen

CABLE AND SUNDRY TOILET WARES.

1 Kitchen Soap
2 Soap Slab, Square
3 Deep Ribbed Soap
4 Hanging Soap
5 Fast Drainer Soap
6 Soap Slab, Oval

7 Cable Brush Vase
8 Cable Mug
9 Male Urinal
10 Female Urinal
11 Cable Covered Soap
12 Newell Spittoon

13 Low Parlor Spittoon
14 Grant Spittoon
15 Cable Chamber
16 Cospadore
17 Bed Pan
18 Burley Spittoon

19 Lincoln Spittoon
20 Cable Ewer and Basin
21 Cable Slop Pail
22 Lenox Combinet
23 Monterey Combinet
24 Catalina Ewer and Basin

Cable and Sundry shapes from a 1916 Homer
Laughlin China Company catalog.

Cable shape jug, white undecorated. $30-35

Cable shape jug, "Pink 'n Yellow Rose" decoration. $50-75

Cable mug, "Pink Rose" decoration. $40-45

Carnival 1938

Carnival was made in solid colors of gray, light green, dark green, turquoise, cobalt, red, ivory and yellow. Carnival was a short line of Quaker Oats premiums found in boxes of Mothers Oats.

Known Carnival pieces: actual measurements

Cup
Saucer 5 1/2"
Bowl small fruit 5 1/2"
Bowl cereal 6 1/8"
Plate 6 1/2"

Carson-Wishmaker

see Andover

Casualstone 1970-1972

The Casualstone Fiesta® line was introduced in 1970 exclusively for the supermarket continuity programs. It was produced under the trade name "Coventry". The glaze is referred to as Antique Gold and has darker gold stamped designs on flatware while the hollowware is a solid Antique Gold color. See also page 59.

Known Casualstone pieces: actual measurements
Decorated
Butter dish
Plate pie
Plate deep 8"
Plate 6"
Plate dinner 10"
Plate salad 7"
Platter oval 13"
Relish tray 13" with
        metal handle
Saucer decorated and
        undecorated

Undecorated
Ashtray
Bowl dessert
Bowl round vegetable
Bowl soup/cereal
Casserole covered
Coffee server
Cream
Marmalade
Mug jumbo
Salt and Pepper shaker
set
Sauceboat
Sugar covered
Tea server

Carnival cups and saucers. $10-15 each set

Casualstone. Courtesy of the Homer Laughlin
China Collectors Association.

Cavalier 1953

Mr. Don Schreckengost designed the
Cavalier (Eggshell) shape in 1953. Cavalier
was designed to fill a need for a more formal
type of ware like the Nautilus Eggshell and
Georgian Eggshell. The Cavalier shape
proved to be very popular and was sold to
many distributors for several years. The
Cavalier shape will be found marked with
company names other than Homer Laughlin.
The Cunningham and Pickett mark on Cavalier is a good example.

Known Cavalier pieces:
   actual measurements
Plate dinner 10"
Plate breakfast 9"
Salad square
Salad or Pie plate 7"
Plate bread and butter 6"
Tea cup and saucer
A.D. cup and saucer
Sauce or Gravy boat
Pitcher cream
Sugar covered
Salt and Pepper
Casserole covered
Bowl rim soup 8"
Bowl fruit 5"
Bowl round vegetable 8 1/2"
Bowl cereal soup 5 1/2"
Platter oval 15"
Platter oval 13"
Platter oval 11"
Platter small 9"
pickle and/or sauceboat stand
Teapot and cover

Right:
Cavalier shapes

sheer elegance
in cavalier egg-shell
semi-porcelain

DINNERWARE

edged in

priceless

PLATINUM

master-crafted
by world renowned

HOMER LAUGHLIN

GUARANTEED OPEN STOCK

ROMANCE

We're proud to present you with these 8 award-winning nationally advertised patterns by famous Homer Laughlin . . . world's largest manufacturer of fine semi-porcelain dinnerware. Each lovely piece is TRIPLE SELECTED . . . GUARANTEED FOREVER against CHECKING OR CRAZING. Each gracious piece is COMPLETELY OVEN-PROOF . . . you may bake in them and serve right to your table. Choose from service for 6, 8 or 12 . . . all patterns available in the banquet *compositions shown on the reverse of this page.*

ROMANCE—So smart . . . so new. Dainty and delicate pastel leaves dotted with pink buds grace the full turquoise rim band. Here's real elegance with PLATINUM edging and stunning Cavalier shape.

BARCLAY

PERSIAN GARDEN

SPRING SONG

BARCLAY—Delightfully refreshing. You'll adore the everlasting beauty of the bud pink band framed with PLATINUM edge lines on Cavalier shape. Center has pretty pink flowers with stylized grey leaves and stems.

PERSIAN GARDEN—An award-winning modern adaptation of a famed Prince's royal design. Equally at home with traditional, provincial or modern decor. Wide teal green band accented with PLATINUM. Cavalier Eggshell.

SPRING SONG—Softly delicate . . . elegantly sophisticated. A perfect blend of turquoise and grey with that just right touch of scarlet. The choice of America's most discriminating hostesses. PLATINUM edge of course. Cavalier shape.

See other side for set composition.

Opposite page:
Homer Laughlin China Company color advertisement showing, upper, Romance in Blue decoration number CV-67 (also called White Oak when sold to Hudson Company in 1956) and lower, Barclay decoration number CV-39, Persian Garden CV-28, Spring Song CV-49.

Cavalier shape plate, Crinoline decoration number CV-5 called Gray Dawn when sold to Cunningham and Pickett. $10-12

Left: Cavalier shape plate, Jade Rose decoration number CV-4 for Lifetime China, Burgundy. $10-12
Cavalier shape plate. $10-12
dark green band, covered sugar and cream. $20-25 set

Cavalier shape covered sugar and cream, Cameo decoration. $20-25 set

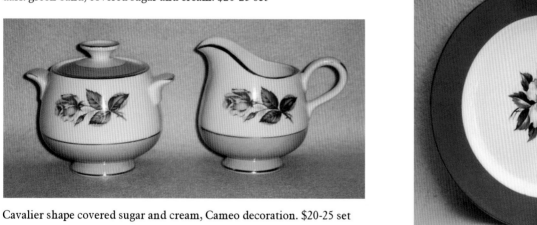

Cavalier shape plate, made for Century Service, Empire Green decoration number CSC-15. Empire Green was also sold to other companies. $10-12

Cavalier shape square luncheon plate, Empire Green decoration number CSC-15. $12-15
teapot $30-35
cream $10-12
sugar $10-12
cup and saucer $8-10

Cavalier shape saucers, Gold Crown decoration. $2-3
Sunrise decoration. $2-3

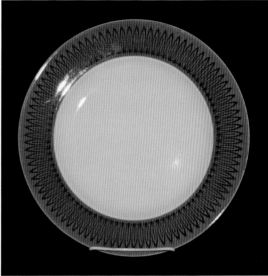

Cavalier shape plate brown border, decoration number CV-142. $8-10

Cavalier shape plate, decoration number CV-90. $8-10

Cavalier shape plate, dark green band Lexington decoration number CV-6. $10-12

Cavalier shape plate with platinum trim, decoration number CV-114. $8-10

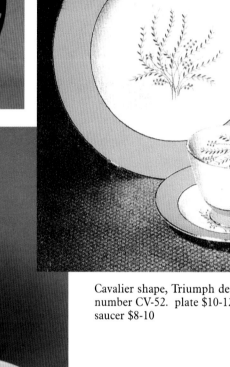

Cavalier shape, Regal Red decoration for the Century Service Corporation. plate $10-12 saucer $2-3

Cavalier shape, Triumph decoration number CV-52. plate $10-12 cup/saucer $8-10

Cavalier shape, Magnolia (gray band) decoration number CV-4. Also called Mango when sold to John Plain Company in 1954, and in 1956 was called Camelia also for John Plain. cup and saucer $8-10
plate $10-12
small bowl $6-10

Right:
Cavalier shape, Spring Song (pink band) decoration number CV-49. dinner plate $10-12
saucer/cup $8-10

Cavalier shape, Lupine decoration number CV-14 also called Trillium Flower. bowl $4-6
small plate $4-6
cup $6-8

Cavalier shape teapot, decoration called Viking for International D.S. also called Royal Harvest. $25-30
Jubilee shape salt and pepper shakers $10-15 pr.
Cavalier small plate $6-8

Cavalier shape covered casserole, Gold Crown decoration for Lifetime China. $25-30
Rhythm shape dinner plate $6-8
small plates $4-6
Cavalier cup and saucer $6-8 set

Cavalier shape, Cottonwood decoration. cup/saucer set, $6-8
plate $6-8
bowl $4-6

Cavalier shape, Pink Radiance decoration from a Homer Laughlin China Company advertisement.

Celeste 1959

Celeste is not a shape but a mixed shaped set made up of the Brittany and Cavalier shapes. Celeste was sold to The Great Atlantic and Pacific Tea Company and several other premium companies. The Celeste decoration is number B-1447, pieces are marked only Celeste.

Known pieces in the Celeste decoration: actual measurements

Brittany	Cavalier
Tea cup/saucer	Sugar covered
Plates 10", 8", 5", 4"	Cream
Plate deep soup 6"	Teapot covered
Fruit 4"	Casserole covered
Nappy 7"	
	Rhythm
	Sauceboat

Celeste backstamp

Cavalier shape, Celeste decoration number LTC21 sold to Lifetime China. only mark "Celeste." Left to right, Covered casserole $25-30
platter $12-15
small bowl $3-4

Centennial 1876

Joseph Chetwynd, an independent decorator for the Homer Laughlin China Company, designed the Centennial shape for the 1876 Philadelphia Exposition where it won an award for serviceable body and glaze. No example of the Centennial shape is available at this time.

Century 1931

The Century shape was introduced in 1931 and the first decorated ware was introduced in November of 1932. Frederick Rhead designed the rectangular shape, which was quite different from the dinnerware shapes that had been previously produced by the Homer Laughlin China Company. Dr. A.V. Bleininger developed the rich ivory vellum glaze. Century was a popular movie give away and advertising shape. In 1938, Century shapes were dipped in solid color glazes of red, yellow, light green and blue (never called mauve blue) and called Riviera.

Known pieces made in the Century shape: trade measurements

Tea cup	Jug 42s covered 5/8 pint
Saucer	Cream
Baker 6", 7", 8"	Sugar and cover
Bowl 36s	Sauce boats, regular and fast stand
Bowl fruit 4"	Teapot 1 1/4 pints
Nappies 6", 7", 8"	Egg cup double
Plate soup 6"	Egg cup
Plates 4", 5", 6", 7", 8"	Casserole
Dishes platters 7", 8"	Butter covered
Pickle	Muffin cover and 7" plate
Jug 36s 6 1/4" tall	
Jug 24s covered 2 1/2 pints	

Century shape sugar, Briar Rose decoration number C-1. $15-18

Century shape plate, Columbine decoration number W331.
$12-14

Century shape covered sugar, decoration number C-2.
$18-20

Century shape plate, Della Robia decoration. $12-14

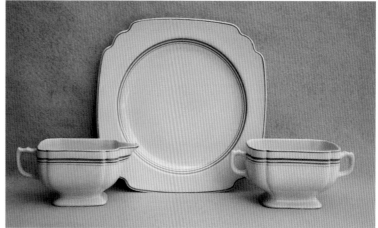

Century shape, decoration number C-135. cream $14-16
plate $12-14
open sugar $10-12

Century shape plate, English Garden decoration
number C-4 also called Old Garden. $12-14

Decoration number C-165. Platter $15-20
cup $10-12

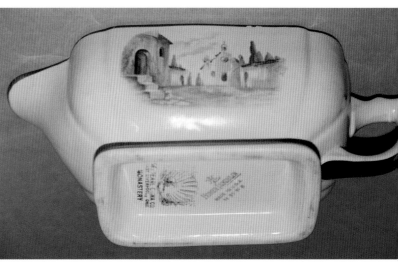

Century shape baker, decoration number MS-81. $20-25

Century shape sauce/gravy boat, Monastery decoration-Pearl China Company. $20-25

Century shape tea pot, single pink rose decoration number C-21. $35-40

Left to right: Century shapes, small plates Arizona decoration number C-223, Hacienda decoration number C-237, Mexicana decoration number C-228, not show Mexicana blue band decoration number C-229, Conchita decoration no number $10-15 each.

Century shape plates from the Homer Laughlin China Company morgue. Top row left to right: English Garden decoration number C-4, rust tulip decoration number C-6, gold trim decoration number C-15, flower spray decoration number C-17, single rose decoration number C-21, green vine decoration number C-23, Bottom row: floral decoration one large two smaller C-28, Rose Spray-decoration number C-29, one large pink floral spray and two smaller flowers-decoration number C-33. No price established on morgue items.

Top row left to right: Century shape, single spray of pink flowers decoration number C-61, single spray of flowers decoration number C-64, green vine decoration number C-65, Bottom row: yellow daisy type flower decoration number C-71, red deco type flower decoration number C-72, two birds and a basket of flowers decoration number C-73. No price established on morgue items.

Century Ivory glaze plates, Top left to right: pastel tulip decoration number C-202, pink floral decoration number C-204, pink floral decoration number C-205, Bottom: rust tulip decoration number C206, four corner floral decoration number C-207. No price established on morgue items.

Century shape plates, floral decoration number C-41, gold border with gold center decoration number C-45, flower four corner decoration number C-48. No price established on morgue items.

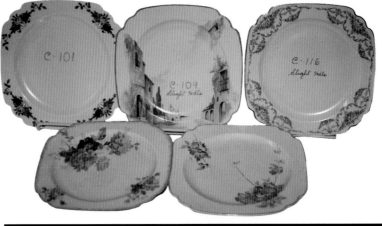

Century shape plates, top row left to right: tulip decoration number C-77, floral decoration number C-79, pink floral decoration number C-82, Middle row: pink floral decoration number C-84, single spray decoration number C-87, floral spray and sprig decoration number C-94. Bottom row: single rose and sprig decoration number C-95, Morningside decoration number C-97. No price established on morgue items.

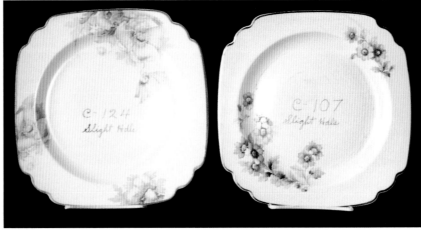

Ivory glaze Century shape plates from the HLC morgue. Top row left to right: cluster of flowers decoration number C-101, decoration number C-109, pink floral/gold garland decoration number C-116 Bottom row: bright orange and rust floral decoration number C-129, Briar Rose decoration number C-1. No price established on morgue items.

From the morgue, Century shape plates, left decoration number C-124, right C107. No price available

Ivory glaze Century shape cream, Sunporch decoration number KK-332, $20-25
go-with tumbler with Sunporch decoration, not made by the Homer Laughlin China Company. No price established

Century shape baker, gold decorative band decoration number C-39. $20-25
cream $14-18
covered sugar $18-24

Left:
Century shape platter, two green lines on ends (would be a different number). $30-35
Jugs are decoration number C-70. Large $125-150, small $70-80

Century 1960's and 1970s

A later and entirely different Century shape was designed in the 1960s. It has no relation to the earlier Century shape except the name.

Known pieces made in the later Century shape: trade measurements
Cup
Saucer
Plates 5",6",8"
Bowl fruit 4"
Bowl coupe soup 6",7"

Later Century shape (no relation to the earlier Century) Left to right: Century shape, Pandora decoration number C-400, right Nordic decoration number C-364 described as Aztec Ring and sold to Sears. They shared the same colored hollowware and only the flatware was decorated. Only the flatware is the Century shape.

Pandora
C-400

Nordic
C-364

Century Service Corporation 1953-1968

The Century Service Corporation was one of the sales organizations of the Cunningham and Pickett group of Alliance, Ohio.

Challenger 1974

The Challenger shape was first made for Block China Company. The design was a collaborative effort of Dennis Newbury and Jerry Gullata of the Block China Company. It was a very difficult shape to execute. The shape did not work out for the Block Company and it was sold to the Jepcor Company. This 1970s shape has narrow edge bands, single line stamp and a narrow mid band. It has a glaze on glaze technique, decorated with and without center decals.

Known Challenger pieces: actual measurements

Bowl cereal/soup	Bowl vegetable 8 1/8"
Plate chop	Sugar covered
Plate dinner 10"	Creamer
Plate salad 5"	Casserole covered
Plate salad 7 1/4"	Butter covered
Cup coffee	Mug
Saucer	Salt and pepper
Sauceboat and stand	

THE NEW AND EXCITING CHALLENGER SHAPE MFG. BY HOMER LAUGHLIN CHINA FOR JEPCOR INTER'L.

Challenger shapes from Homer Laughlin catalog

Challenger shape, Creamy White decoration. cream $6-8
plate $6-8
covered sugar $8-10

Challenger shape. This was one of two decorations made for Graham Kerr, the Galloping Gourmet.
dinner plate $25-30,
cup/saucer $10-15 set,
small plate $10-12.

Charm House 1950

Don Schreckengost designed the Charm House shape hollow ware released in 1950. The first shapes were exclusive decorations for the United China and Glass Company. The Charm House shape is hollowware only and is usually found in solid colors, although decals were also applied. The solid colors of brown, black, dark green, yellow, chartreuse and bright blue were used with the Applique and also the Dura Print lines. Some solid color Charm House pieces were also used with the Kenilworth shape.

Known pieces made in the Charm House shape: trade measurements

Tea cup	Salt and Pepper
Sugar covered	Sauceboat
Cream	Nappy 7"
Casserole covered	Nappy 8"
Cereal soup	A.D. cup
Teapot covered	

Charm House Lotus Hai CH-106 advertisement

Drawing for Charm House shapes, Lotus Hai

Charm House Pink Magnolia CH-100.

Chateau Buffet

Chateau Buffet was produced for the Quaker Oats Company as a give away premium in boxes of their cereal. The Taylor Smith and Taylor Pottery Company shared in the production of Chateau Buffet.

Known Chateau Buffet pieces:
Custard
French casserole
Oval baker
Pie dish individual

Mother's Oats box. Chateau Buffet made for Quaker Oats. small fruit bowl $3-4, custard bowl $3-4

Chelsea 1886

Chelsea was a translucent, vitrified porcelain or china and was designed by Elijah Chetwynd in early 1886. It was produced in a full line of thin dinnerware and tea services as well as water jugs, trays and beakers. Old trade journals describe the body as the color of milk, neither white nor cream, with a fragile eggshell like quality. It was the first shape to use the Laughlin horseshoe back stamp. The Laughlin horseshoe backstamp was only used on china made from 1886 to 1889.

1886 Chelsea shape decoration unidentified sauceboat $15-20 open sugar $15-20.

Chelsea 1934

The Chelsea shape was a product of the early 1930s and in all probability was co-produced with other potteries to fill large orders for companies like Quaker Oats.

1934 Chelsea platter, decoration same as (Wells) W5623. $30-35

1930s Chelsea shape, no identification available.
Left to right: small plate $8-10
saucer $4-6   saucer $4-6
plate $8-10   saucer $4-6

1930s Chelsea shape platter, decoration number CH28. $25-30

1930s Chelsea shape vegetable bowl, decoration number (appears to be) CH04. $20-25

Chelsea shape plate, Wild Rose Bouquet decoration. $14-16

Chelsea shape plate, Poppy Flower decoration.
$14-16

Club Aluminum

See Household Institute

Colonial late 1800s - early 1900s

The Colonial Shape was released prior to the turn of the 19th century. Other shapes were used in the Colonial line. The first three items on the top row are the Danube shape individual sugar, teapot, and individual cream, items 16 through 19 are the Geisha shape, the cups are Golden Gate, Ovide and Rococo shape. Only cup #26 is the Colonial shape. The Alaska and Newport shapes are also used in this Colonial set. In a 1901 catalog the American Beauty bowl was used in the Colonial set composition.

Colonial backstamp

Colonial shape plate, decoration number 4570.
plate $16-18

Chelsea shape oval vegetable bowl, decoration number CH51, $15-20
saucer, same decoration as W5923. $4-6

Items shown are from a 1901 Homer Laughlin China Company catalog

Top Row: Item 1-individual sugar, Item 2-individual teapot, Item 3-individual cream, Item 4- after dinner coffee, Item 5-sugar, Item 6-teapot, Item 7-cream, Item 8-jug, Item 9-sauce boat, Item 10-pickle dish.

Row 2: Item 11-coupe soup, Item 12-fruit, Item 13-individual butter, Item 14- egg cup, Item 15- spooner, Item 16- Geisha sugar, Item 17- Geisha teapot, Item 18- Geisha cream, Item 19- Geisha jug, Item 20- nappy, Item 21- baker

Row 3: Item 22- oatmeal, Item 23- Golden Gate tea, Item 24- Ovide tea, Item 25-Rococo tea, Item 26- Colonial coffee, Item 27- Colonial tea, Item 28- bouillon cup, Item -29 bowl

Row 4: Item 30- covered butter, Item 31- Alaska ice cream, Item 32- cake plate, Item 33-dish (platter), Item 34- plate 7", Item 35- deep soup plate, Item 36- Newport bowl

Row 5: Item 37- oyster tureen, Item 38- casserole, Item 39- sauce tureen complete, Item 40- covered dish, Item 41- soup tureen complete

Colonial shape sauceboat, Chrysanthemum decoration. $18-24

Colonial shape plate, decoration number 4727. $16-18

Colonial shape platter, decoration number 23. $18-24

Colonial shape casserole lid only,
Colonial Violet. $15-18

Colonial shape platter, Colonial Violet decoration. $25-30

Colonial White

See Dover

Color Tone

Color Tone was more of a promotional name than a shape or a process. It seems to be a continuation of the Dura-Print process and was more than likely used on mixed shapes. Shown are Rose Garden, Pink Lady, Diana and Green and Sugar Maple.

Color Tone 1960s Homer Laughlin China Company advertisement showing Rose Garden, Pink Lady, Diana, Green Maple and Sugar Maple decorations in the Color Tone line.

Coronet 1935

Coronet was introduced in 1935 and was designed by Frederick Rhead. It was a popular shape according to trade papers of the time. So popular that the shape was copied by Japanese potters in 1936. Several different decorations were applied to the Coronet shape as well as being produced in Ming Yellow, Old Ivory and Sea Green.

Known pieces made in the Coronet shape: actual measurements
Baker
Bowl 5"
Casserole covered
Cream
Dish (platters) 15", 13", 11"
Bowl fruit
Plates 10", 9", 8", 7", 6"
Plate deep soup
Pickle
Sauceboat and stand
Sugar covered
Tea cup
Tea saucer

Coronet shape backstamp

Coronet shape plates, left decoration number CO-57, right CO-58, plates $14-16 each

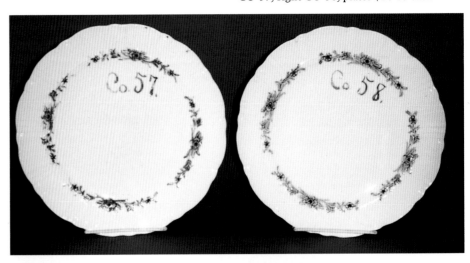

Coronet shape, Greenbriar decoration number CO-532,
left to right, plate $10-12
small plate $6-8
cream $8-10
cup $6-8

Coronet shape, Chintz decoration number CO-115. small
plate $6-8
plate $10-12
cup/saucer $10-12 set

JUNE ROSE PATTERN

Refreshing and lovely as roses in June, this delightful, new pattern is fully as charming as the name suggests. Designed in the very newest shape, it displays against the popular ivory body a beautiful spray of large, pink and white roses and buds, interspersed with blue flowers and green leaves. The whole is most attractively set off by a lovely, embossed border. It is a set which you will never tire, appropriate for every occasion. Its durability permits you to enjoy it in everyday use.

Size of Set	32-pc.	51-pc.
Number	1423	1430
For COUPONS	$9.00	$16.00
Mlg. wt.	18 lbs.	34 lbs.

32 Pc. $9 COUPON VALUE

Premiums 125

1930s advertisement for June
Rose decoration on the Coronet
shape

Coronet shape saucer, June Rose decoration. $3-4

Coronet shape, Pink Castles decoration. plate $12-14
cream $10-12

Coronet shape, small plates, left to right Petit Point decoration, Nova
Flower decoration number CO-257. $8-10 each.

Coronet shape sauce boat, Platinum Wreath decoration.
$12-15

Coronet shape, Wildflowers decoration. small plate $8-10
lug soup $10-12

Coventry Casualstone

see Casualstone

Homer Laughlin advertisement for Coventry Casualstone dinnerware.

Craftsman 1934

The Craftsman line was introduced in the Gold Room of the Fort Pitt Hotel in Pittsburgh and the Stevens Hotel in Chicago January 8, 1934. The initial offering, under the Craftsman trademark was the Georgian shape with its brilliant craze proof texture and elaborate decorations. The Georgian regular shape was patent number 345,141 filed December 20,1933. (See Georgian Regular)

Cunningham Industries 1958-1960s

Cunningham Industries was part of the Cunningham and Pickett operation of Alliance, Ohio.

Cunningham & Pickett backstamp

Cunningham and Pickett 1938-1960s

The Cunningham and Pickett Company of Alliance, Ohio was a major distributor of Homer Laughlin China from 1938 into the 1960s. Their business was primarily grocery store continuity (premium) lines. It has been estimated that Cunningham and Pickett purchased about 90% of their premium dinnerware line from the Homer Laughlin China Company. If you would like more information about the Cunningham and Pickett operation see *Homer Laughlin, the 1940s and 1950s* also published by the Schiffer Publishing Company.

Currier and Ives

see Americana

Currier and Ives 1970s

Another Currier and Ives decoration was made for the Kingsway China Company of Alliance, Ohio. The Kingsway Company was also part of the Cunningham and Pickett organization.

Brittany shape, Currier and Ives decoration made for Kingsway, Alliance, Ohio. plate $8-10
saucer $2-3
cup $4-6

Daisy Chain 1933

The first mention of the Daisy Chain shape was found in the old records in 1933. It was a bake and serve line with a chain like embossed decoration directly under the outer rim. By 1937 fourteen different decorations were offered on Daisy Chain.

Known Daisy Chain pieces:
Plate pie
Plate cake
Casserole covered

Backside of pie baker showing Daisy Chain decoration.

Daisy Chain shape pie plate, Petit Point decoration. $30-35

Daisy Chain shape pie baker, Kitchen Bouquet decoration. $25-30

Daisy Chain shape bowl and cover, decoration number MW-67. $30-35

Daisy Chain shape covered casserole. Same as OS-150 decoration. $30-35

Daisy Chain casserole and cover, decoration number DC701. $30-35

Daisy Chain bowl, decoration number DC 715. $18-24

Daisy Chain shape covered casserole. Same as N-260 decoration. $30-35

Daisy Chain covered casserole, Handy Andy body, Daisy Chain decoration around rim instead of rings. $45-50
These share the decoration OS-126:
cake plate $20-25
pie baker $25-30
server $25-30

Daisy Chain covered bowl. This may have been sold to Royal Metal Manufacturing Company as it matches the description on one of their orders. Marked Oven Serve. $55-65

Daisy Chain bowl and cover, Gold Star decoration. $30-35

Danube 1893

The Danube shape is a three piece porcelain tea set that won an award at the Chicago World's Fair in 1893. The Homer Laughlin manufacturer mark is an American Eagle over the British lion. The set consists of an individual size teapot, sugar and cream. The individual Danube tea set was later offered as part of the Colonial dinnerware set.

Danube shape, Individual teapot, cream and sugar, decoration not known. The individual cream and the teapot are marked with the Eagle over the Lion backstamp. The covered sugar in this particular set is marked "Colonial." set $300

Debutante 1950

The Debutante shape was introduced in 1950 and is the same shape as Jubilee. The special snow-white glaze is a perfect background for colorful decorative treatments. Don Schreckengost designed the Debutante shape.

Known pieces made in the Debutante shape: actual measurements

Tea cup and saucer   Chop plate 15"
Plate 10"   Salt and Pepper shaker set
Plate 9"   Coffee pot covered
Plate 7"   Tea pot covered
Plate 6"
Soup coupe 8"
Soup lug
Bowl fruit 5 1/2"
Platter 11"
Platter 13"
Platter 15"
Nappy 7 1/2"
Nappy 8 1/2"
Sauceboat, Fast Stand
Casserole covered
Sugar covered
Cream

Flame Flower
PATTERN NO. D-8 PRICE LIST

1. Tea Cup	$_____
2. Tea Saucer	_____
3. Plate, 10"	_____
4. Plate, 9"	_____
5. Plate, 7"	_____
6. Plate, 6"	_____
7. Coupe Soup, 8"	_____
8. Lug Soup	_____
9. Fruit, 5½"	_____
10. Platter, 11"	_____
11. Platter, 13"	_____
12. Platter, 15"	_____
13. Nappie, 7½"	_____
14. Nappie, 8½"	_____
15. Sauceboat, Fast Stand	_____
16. Casserole, Cov'd.	_____
17. Sugar, Cov'd.	_____
18. Cream	_____
19. Chop Plate, 15"	_____
20. Salt Shaker	_____
21. Pepper Shaker	_____
22. Coffee Pot, Cov'd.	_____
23. Tea Pot, Cov'd.	_____
24. Coffee Cup, A.D.	_____
25. Coffee Saucer, A.D.	_____
STARTER SETS	
20 Pc. AT (with fruits)	_____
20 Pc. BT (with lug soups)	_____

The Homer Laughlin China Co.
NEWELL, WEST VIRGINIA
Printed in U.S.A.

Debutante shapes from a Homer Laughlin brochure.

Debutante shape plates, left Sequence decoration on white body, right Sequence decoration SR 121 on blue body. $10-12 each

Left:
Debutante shape plate, Cattail decoration number D-2. $10-12

Debutante shape cream, Violets decoration number MW-181. $8-10

Debutante shape small plate, Wild Grape decoration number D-5. $4-6

Debutante shape plate, Violets decoration number MW-181. $8-10

Debutante shape, Windsor Rose decoration.
plate $8-10
cream $6-8
sugar covered $8-10

Debutante shape plate, Flame Flower decoration number D-8. $8-10

Debutante shape, Hawaii decoration from June 1951 trade publication.

Debutante shape plate, Hawaii decoration. $8-10

Debutante shape, Gray Laurel decoration from July 1950 trade publication.

Debutante shape, Dogwood decoration number D-3

Debutante shape, Bali Flower decoration. $8-10

Debutante shape, Champagne decoration. From an old trade journal.

Debutante shape plate, Bali Flower decoration. $8-10

Doric 1936

Doric is a short set consisting of solid white cup, saucer and plate, which were produced for Quaker Oats in 1936. Shape names of Modern or Corinthian were considered before settling on Doric.

Dover 1970s

The shape is a 1970s octagonal paneled shape in greens, browns, Colonial White, and Colonial White with decorations. All of the colors in the Dover shape were given the designation of CW for Colonial White. Colonial White is CW-100.

Known pieces made in the Dover shape:

Sugar covered
Cream
Plate bread and butter
Plate salad
Plate dinner
Platter round
Tray relish
Cup/saucer
Coffee server covered

Teapot covered
Bowl vegetable
Bowl soup/cereal
Bowl soup/large
Bowl dessert/fruit
Casserole covered
Tureen covered and ladle
Butter covered 1/4 lb.
Sauceboat

Doric shape plate $4-6, cup $5-6, saucer $1-2

Homer Laughlin advertisement showing the Dover shape in Colonial White undecorated.

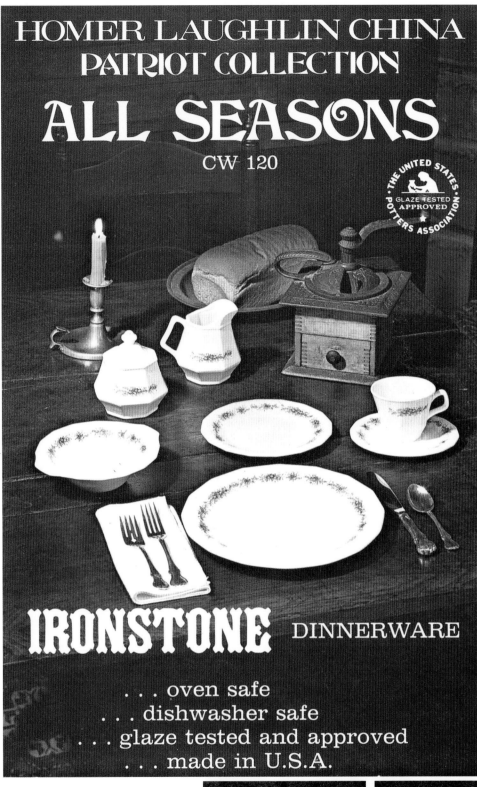

HOMER LAUGHLIN CHINA
PATRIOT COLLECTION
ALL SEASONS
CW 120

THE UNITED STATES · GLAZE TESTED APPROVED · POTTERS ASSOCIATION

IRONSTONE DINNERWARE

... oven safe
... dishwasher safe
... glaze tested and approved
... made in U.S.A.

Homer Laughlin advertisement Dover shape. All Seasons decoration number CW-120.

Dover shape, Homespun decoration number CW-102, Blue Onion decoration number CW-104 and Bay Berry decoration number CW-105.

Homespun CW-102

Blue Onion CW-104

Bay Berry CW-105

Dover shape Bicentennial plate $10-15.

Dover shape Avocado Green plate, called Ardmore when sold to Sears, decoration number CW-115. $5-6

Dover shape, Colonial White, Floribunda decoration number CW-128 and Mary Lloyd decoration number CW-131.

Left:
Dover shape sugar (lid missing), Bayberry decoration number CW-105. If complete $8-10

Right:
Dover shape plate, Dover Rose decoration number CW-117. $5-6

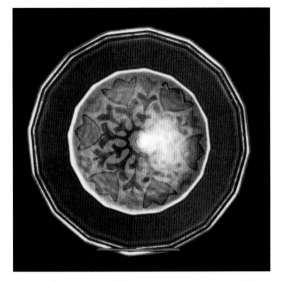

Dover shape plate, Tulip decoration number CW-124, made for Jepcor's Wilshire House line. $5-6

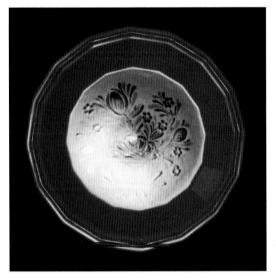

Dover shape plate, Floribunda/Bouquet decoration number CW-128, sold to Newcor and Wards. $5-6

Dura-Print

Dura-Print is a unique process which combined a number of printing techniques to achieve new and interesting decorative effects which were not possible with usual decorating methods. The process allowed designs to be printed directly on white ware under glaze, giving a textured appearance. Even though Dura-Print is a decorating process it appears as a back stamp usually on coupe and curved surfaces. Solid color glazes are designated as B-Black, BL-Blue, BR-Brown, CH-Chartreuse, DG-Dark Green, and Y-Yellow.

Dura-Print decorated items on Rhythm shape: actual measurements

Plate 10"
Plate 9"
Plate 7"
Plate 5"
Plate 6"
Bowl fruit 4"
Soup coupe 8"
Nappie 8 1/2"
Platter 11 1/2"
Platter 13 1/2"
Pickle 9"

Dura-Print colored glaze items on Rhythm shape:

Tea cup and saucer
Sugar covered
Cream
Casserole covered
Soup/cereal
Salt and pepper
Tea pot covered
Sauceboat regular

Dura-Print line, Rhythm shape flatware, Charm House hollow ware, Something Blue decoration with solid blue hollow ware. Back platter $15-20, cup/saucer set $10-12, Cream $12-14, Sugar and cover $14-16

Charm House shape Dura-Print line green teapot. $25-30

Charm House shape Dura-Print line saucer/cup. Wheat Americana decoration for Krogers. $8-10 set

This exciting new DURA-PRINT pattern—in Blue Spruce Green and Chestnut Brown—adds a gay note of spring, the year 'round, to America's smartest tables.

Pittsburgh China and Pottery Show – Hotel William Penn – Rooms 403-405-407.

The Homer Laughlin China Co.
NEWELL, WEST VIRGINIA

JANUARY 1953 CHINA, GLASS AND DECORATIVE ACCESSORIES

Homer Laughlin advertisement for the Dura-Print line with Trellis decoration.

This smart, new, gay informal dinnerware features interesting textural underglaze pattern in contemporary color combinations—accented by solid-colored, smooth-flowing hollow ware, "HIGHLAND PLAID," made with Homer Laughlin's new DURA-PRINT process.

Highland Plaid

Below:
Dura-Print line, Rhythm shape platter, Calypso decoration. $15-18

Dura-Print plate, Daybreak decoration (called Chanticleer by Sears). $10-12

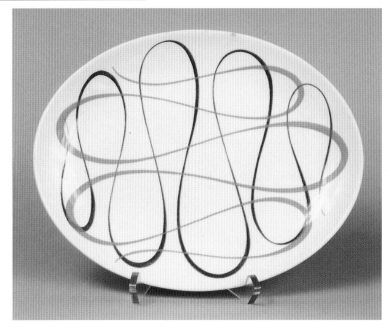

Homer Laughlin advertisement Dura-Print line, Polka-Print decoration.

Polka-Print

This lovely new Dura-Print pattern captures a sophisticated charm with its dainty black polka dots geometrically placed against a creamy white background. Further enhanced by the contrasting smooth black hollo-ware, POLKA-PRINT lends a note of refreshing simplicity to any table. New, distinctive table top fashion at conservative prices.

Eastern Sales and Display Room: Suite 2000, 212 Fifth Ave., New York 10, N. Y. • Bernard Menge
Chicago Sales Office: Room 916, LaSalle-Wacker Bldg., 221 No. LaSalle St., Chicago 1, Ill. • Norman W. MacDonald

The Homer Laughlin China Co.
NEWELL, WEST VIRGINIA

Dura-Print line Debutante shape Malay decoration. $10-12

Dura-Print saucers, Plaid decoration with Charm House hollow ware. Cream $4-6, Cup and saucer set $4-6

Duratone 1960s

The Duratone shape is a 1960s mixed short set of Studio and other hollowware combined with Rhythm flatware.

Listed are known pieces made in the Duratone line: actual measurements
Tea cup, Studio shape
Tea saucer
Plate, dinner 10"
Plate, luncheon 9"
Plate, salad/pie 7"
Plate 6"
Soup, coupe 7 1/2"
Cereal 6"
Fruit/dessert 5 1/4"
Platter 13 1/2", 11 1/2"
Vegetable dish round 8 1/2"
Sugar/cover, Studio shape
Cream, Studio shape
Sauceboat
Pickle/relish dish
Tea pot/cover
Salt/pepper shakers
Casserole/cover, Studio shape

Homer Laughlin advertisement for Duratone line Blue Wheat decoration number RU-509.

Homer Laughlin advertisement for Duratone line Black Eyed Susan decoration number RU-505.

Homer Laughlin advertisement for Duratone line Buttercup decoration number RU-506.

Duratone

**ALL OCCASION
DETERGENT PROOF**

TANTALIZE . . . A new warm brown proudly encircles delicate spring fronds touched off with saucy, gay blossoms to tantalize the latest underglaze, dishwasher and oven-proof dinnerware. The hint of warmth lends itself gracefully to entertaining.
Pattern RU-510

The **HOMER LAUGHLIN CHINA COMPANY**

Homer Laughlin advertisement for Duratone line, Tantalize decoration number RU-510.

Duratone line. Spring Garden decoration. plate $8-10
cup $4-6
saucer $1-2

SPECIAL OFFER!!
3 PIECE PLACE SETTING ONLY
99¢
cup-saucer
10" dinner plate
EXQUISITE NEW
Spring Garden
BY HOMER LAUGHLIN.

Box showing 3-piece place setting
for 99 cents. Box $8-10

Early American Homes

Early American Homes is a difficult-to-find decoration and was sold to the J.C. Penney Company in 1940. The set was made up of the Brittany, Willow and Empress shape. Early American Homes, Americana and the Historical American Subjects each have a different border.

Known items made in Early American Homes: trade measurements

Plate 7"	Brittany	Mt. Vernon
Plate 4"	Brittany	Abe Lincoln's home
Cup	Willow	Paul Revere home
Saucer	Willow	Robert E. Lee home
Bowl fruit 4"	Empress	Thomas Jefferson home
Bowl oatmeal		California Mission
Platter 11"	Brittany	Independence Hall
Platter 11"	Brittany	Mount Vernon
Nappy	Empress	Betsy Ross home

Early American Homes line bowl, Home of Betsy Ross decoration. $20-25

Early American Homes line platter, Independence Hall decoration. $20-25
plate, Mt. Vernon decoration. $18-20
saucer, Arlington decoration. $4-6
fruit bowl, Monticello decoration. $8-10

Empress 1914

The Empress shape was introduced in 1914 and was a popular shape for many years. Empress was made in an undecorated white glaze and white glaze with decorations. It was also produced in solid colors. The Empress shape was advertised as first quality American pure white semi-porcelain in plain edge shape.

Row l: Item 1- teapot, Item 2- sugar, Item 3- cream, Item 4- individual sugar, Item 5 -individual cream, Item 6 -coffee, Item 7- tea, Item 8- After Dinner coffee

Row 2: Item 9- covered butter, Item10 - double handle sauce boat, Item 11- fast stand sauce boat, Item 12- cream soup and stand, Item 13- bouillon cup and saucer, Item 14- ramekin and stand

Row 3: Item 15- nappy 7", Item 16- coupe soup 7", Item 17- oatmeal 36s, Item 18- fruit 4", Item 19- individual butter, Item 20- bone dish, Item 21- bowl 36s, Item 22 -Boston egg cup, Item 23-spoon holder

Row 4: Item 24- dish 10" (platter), Item 25- cake plate, Item 26- plate 7", Item 27- baker 7", Item 28- pickle

Row 5: Item 29- sauce boat and stand, Item 30- oyster tureen, Item 31- casserole 7", Item 33- sauce tureen complete, Item 34- jug 24s

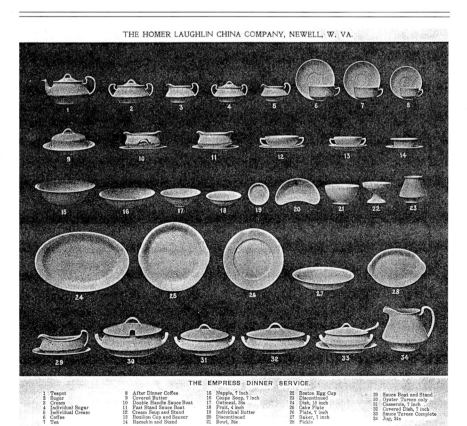

Empress shapes from a Homer Laughlin China Company catalog.

Empress shape sauce/gravy boat, decoration number E-5605. $18-20

Empress shape covered casserole, Gold Band decoration. $30-35

Empress shape sauce/gravy boat, Blue Medallion decoration. $18-20

Empress shape covered butter, Gold Bow Knot decoration number E3906. $75-85

Empress shape, Floral Basket decoration. covered sugar $14-16
small plate $4-6
cream $10-12

Empress shape plate, LaSalle decoration number E-8705. $8-10

Empress shape plate, Oriental Border decoration number E7805. $8-10

Empress shape cream, decoration number E4904. $10-12

Empress shape, Rose and Lattice decoration number E1715. plate $8-10 covered butter $50-65

Empress shape sugar, decoration number E4201. $18-24

Empress shape teapot solid yellow treatment. No price established

Empress shape platter, decoration number E9005. $18-20

Empress shape small plates, left decoration number E or K4613, right Springtime decoration number E2513. $6-8 each

Empress shape covered butter, Springtime decoration number E2513. $50-75

Empress shape covered vegetable dish, decoration number E6704. $30-35

Empress shape small plates left decoration number E or K4713, right decoration number E4513. $6-8 each

Empress shape plates, left decoration number E7113, right Blue Birds and Apple Blossoms decoration number E9303. $10-12 each

Empress shape plates left, decoration number E7507, right decoration number E7413. $10-12 each

Empress shape covered butter, decoration number E or K2015. $50-75

Empress shape platter, decoration number MS81. $20-25

Empress shape jug, Bluebird decoration number E-7413. $40-45

Empress shape plate, decoration number E9205. $8-10

Empress shape covered dish, decoration number E9005. $30-35

Empress shape covered dish, decoration number E7505. $30-35

Empress shape covered casserole, Rose Border decoration number E5205. $30-35

Empress shape covered casserole, Violets decoration number E5204. $30-35

Empress shape covered casserole, Rose Basket decoration number 9810-G-1. $30-35

Epicure 1955

Epicure was introduced in 1955 and advertised as "—an oven-proof, multi-purpose, casual line of dinnerware and serving pieces in four color glazes -Snow White, Dawn Pink, Turquoise Blue and Charcoal Gray". Don Schreckengost designed the Epicure shape.

Known pieces made in the Epicure shape: actual measurements

Plate 10"	Sugar covered
Plate 8"	Coffee pot covered
Plate 6"	Dish covered
Cup coffee and saucer	Nappy covered 8"
Casserole individual covered	Soup coupe 8"
	Soup cereal
Platter 12"	Sauceboat
Pickle	Ladle
Cream	Salt and Pepper

Epicure shape 8" nappy, Dawn Pink $45-50
Salt and Pepper set, Charcoal Gray $20-25
10" dinner plate, Charcoal Gray $20-25
top: Covered casserole, Turquoise Blue $100-125

Epicure shape cup Dawn Pink, rare Turquoise ashtray, sugar bowl (lid missing) Snow White. Back row: Individual covered casserole Turquoise Blue.

Famous Old Ships 1941

The Famous Old Ships series was produced on the Nautilus flatware and the Swing hollowware. Some of the famous old ships in the series were Santa Maria, Mayflower, San Martin, Bounty and the California Clipper. The border is made up of flowers and shells. The picture shown is from the morgue and we have no proof positive that this decoration was actually produced.

Famous Old Ships backstamp.

Nautilus shape, Famous Ships decoration. covered sugar, large round plate. No prices established from morgue items.

Fantasy 1940s

The Fantasy decoration was sold to Montgomery Wards in the early 1940s and was not a successful pattern. Another mixed shape set, the flatware appears to be Brittany, the teacup cream and sugar are the Willow shape. Blue Fantasy is slightly more accessible than the pink. Fantasy is a decoration name and not a shape name. The body of the covered casserole is the Wells shape with a Willow shape knob. The finial on the Fantasy sugar is also the Willow shape.

1941 Montgomery Ward catalog showing the Fantasy decoration on mixed shapes.

Willow shape, Blue Fantasy decoration. Fantasy was also made in pink. covered sugar $18-20
cream $14-18

Fashion 1958

Fashion is a limited hollowware shape made to go along with mixed sets and was sold to the Alliance China Company in 1958. The Fashion shape was designed by Don Schreckengost and is a pared down version of the Epicure shape.

Listed are known pieces in the Fashion shape:
Tea cup
Sugar covered
Cream
Sauceboat

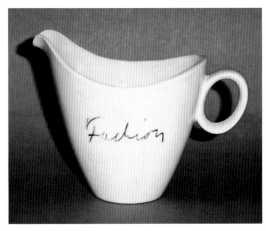

Fashion shape cream, white undecorated. No price established

Fiesta® from a February, 1936 Crockery and Glass Journal heralding the success of the newly released Fiesta®.

Fiesta® 1936

Fiesta® was introduced at the January 1936 trade show in Pittsburgh, Pennsylvania. Frederick Rhead designed the shape and Dr. A.V. Bleininger developed the colorful glazes. The original colors introduced in 1936: red, light green, yellow, turquoise and ivory.

THE SENSATION OF THE SHOW

FIESTA " "

AT the Pottery and Glass Show in Pittsburgh last month one word was on everybody's lips. It was "Fiesta" . . . the name of the sensational new line of pottery in solid colors introduced by Homer Laughlin. Fiesta captured the imagination of the trade . . . instantly . . . at first sight . . . a forecast of the success that Fiesta is destined to achieve with the women of America.

Fiesta is available in five lovely colors . . . Green, Yellow, Blue, Ivory and Red . . . all brilliant, all eye-catching, all modern. Using these colors, a hostess dresses her table to suit the occasion and her own tastes . . . and makes of every meal a celebration. Superbly shaped, of high quality in material and texture, designed and executed with artistic skill, Fiesta is still moderately priced. It offers a wide variety of items from which your customers may choose, and may be bought by the piece.

Investigate Fiesta . . . the pottery sensation of 1936. Find out for yourself the possibilities for . . . fast, repeat profit it extends .. every merchant. We invite you to write us for complete information, prices and descriptive literature.

HOMER LAUGHLIN CHINA COMPANY • NEWELL, W. VA.
Pacific Coast Representative . . . M. Seller Co., San Francisco, Calif., and Portland, Ore.
Chicago Office . . . Room 15-104 Merchandise Mart

PRICE LIST
(Per Piece)

WARE	GREEN BLUE YELLOW OLD IVORY	RED
Tea Cups	$ .20	$ .30
Tea Saucers	.15	.20
Plates—10 inch	.35	.50
— 9 inch	.30	.45
— 7 inch	.25	.35
— 6 inch	.20	.30
Cream Soup Cups	.45	.65
Onion Soups Covered	.65	.90
Fruits—5 inch	.15	.20
Dessert—6 inch	.30	.40
Coffee cups A.D.	.20	.25
Coffee Saucers A.D.	.10	.15
Chop Plates—15 inch	1.00	1.50
Chop Plates—13 inch	.75	1.10
Nappies—9½ inch	.50	.80
—8½ inch	.40	.55
Casseroles Covered	1.40	2.00
Comports—12 inch	1.50	2.25
Comports Sweets—5½ inch	.60	.85
Compartment Plates	.65	1.00
Salad Bowls Footed—12 inch	2.25	1.75
Sugars Covered	.70	1.00
Creamers	.40	.55
Coffee Pot A.D.	1.00	1.40
Coffee Pots Regular	1.25	1.75
Tea Pots Regular	1.25	1.75
Ice Pitchers—2 Quarts	1.35	2.00
Jugs—(5 Pts.)	1.50	2.00
Carafes—3 Pints	1.50	2.00
Vases Bud	.40	.55
Candle Holder Tripods	.65	.85
Candle Holder Bulbs	.40	.50
Ash Trays	.15	.20
Salt Shakers	.25	.40
Pepper Shakers	.25	.40
Relish Trays Complete	1.50	2.25
Egg Cups	.30	.40
Deep Plates—8 inch	.30	.40
Tom and Jerry Mugs	.30	.40
Mustards—Covered	.40	.60
Marmalade Jars—Covered	.65	.90
Utility Trays	.40	.55
Flower Vases— 8 inch	.75	1.00
Flower Vases—10 inch	1.25	1.75
Flower Vases—12 inch	1.75	2.25
Bowls—11½ inch	1.10	1.50
—10 inch	.65	1.00
— 9 inch	.50	.75
— 8 inch	.40	.60
— 7 inch	.35	.50
— 5 inch	.20	.35
Bowl Covers—8 inch	.30	.40
—7 inch	.30	.40
—6 inch	.20	.30
—5 inch	.20	.30

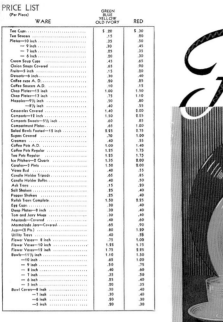

THE HOMER LAUGHLIN CHINA CO., NEWELL, W. VA.

COLOR! That's the trend today . . . a trend that has gained momentum steadily in every department of design and decoration, in every room of our homes. Emphasis is withdrawn from the drab, uninteresting monotones . . . and placed heavily upon brightness, gayety . . . color! It is in this spirit of gayety and color that we offer you Fiesta . . . a new ware that provides endless possibilities for interesting, tasteful and eye-catching color effects in dressing the modern table.

Fiesta comes in five lovely colors . . . Green, Yellow, Blue, Old Ivory and Red . . . all brilliant, all cheerful, all endowed with a pleasant feeling of good fellowship, informality and gracious living. Whether used for serving breakfast, luncheon, informal supper, or buffet, Fiesta makes the meal a truly gay occasion. It gives the hostess an opportunity to create her own table effects by combining, according to her tastes or the occasion, any colors in any way she desires. Plates of one color, cream soups of another, contrasting cups and saucers . . . it's fun to set a table with Fiesta !

Fiesta is superbly shaped, is of high quality both in material and texture, is designed and executed with artistic skill of the first order. It offers a wide variety of items, increasing the possibilities of creating a table ensemble of true color harmony. And although pleasantly reminiscent of the lovely Faience tradition, it is thoroughly modern and different. Best of all, Fiesta is extremely reasonable in price, may be bought by the piece, and thus affords the purchaser a chance to build up a set not only of whatever items, but of whatever colors, she desires.

1937 Fiesta® brochure from a 1937 Butler Brothers catalog.

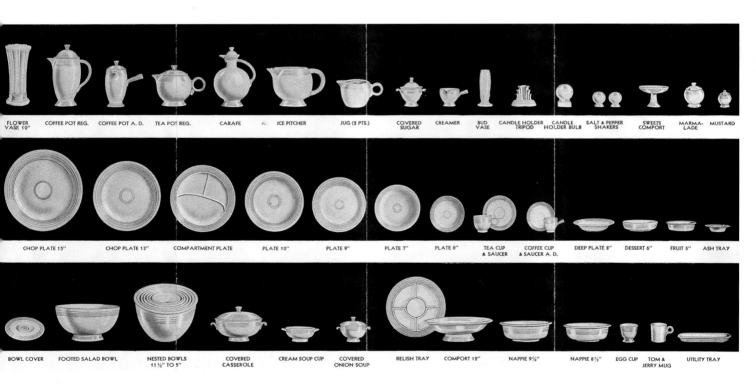

Fiesta shapes from the 1937 brochure attached to the Butler Brothers catalog.

Fiesta® 10" green plate $25-30
9" cobalt blue plate $15-18
7" small ivory plate $8-10
6" red plate $7-8
yellow cup/saucer set $20-24

A 1936 company brochure lists only #1, #2, #3 and #4 bowl lids found in the first five colors. A #7 lid is listed in Frederick Rhead's journal as being modeled but has not as yet been found. Fiesta mixing bowl set lids are extremely hard to find. #1, #2, #3, $700-800 each #4 $850-900
#5 and #6 were found and sold in 1997 for $31,000

A collection of medium green Fiesta® bowls.

Fiesta® Casuals 1960s

Fiesta® Casual China was offered in a 1960s Plaid Stamp catalog in a Daisy decoration (although it was not called Daisy). Hawaiian Daisy decoration has a turquoise band around the edge of the plate and each flower has twelve petals surrounding an Amberstone brown center. The decorated flatware was made to co-ordinate with in stock turquoise Fiesta® hollowware.

Another decoration is called Yellow Carnation by collectors and the decorated flatware was designed to co-ordinate with yellow Fiesta® hollowware. The Carnation has a band of yellow around the edge of the plate. Yellow flowers with brown centers form a circle around the plate's center with brown leaves.

Fiesta ® Casual China plate. $10-15

Known pieces in Fiesta® Casuals: actual measurements
Plates 7", 10"
Platter oval
Saucer

Left, Fiesta ® Casual Hawaiian Daisy small plate $10-15. Right, Fiesta ® Casual Yellow Carnation saucer. $6-8

Page from a 1964 trading stamp catalog showing several Homer Laughlin patterns including Fiesta Casual China. Homer Laughlin patterns shown are item numbers (1) Blue Aster, (2) Barclay on Cavalier, (3) Fiesta® Casual China, (10)Turquoise Melody on Cavalier shape. (Item number 4 is not Homer Laughlin)

Fiesta® Foursome

see Harmony sets

Fiesta® Ironstone 1969-1972

Ironstone Fiesta® was made in three colors, Mango Red, Turf Green and Harvest Gold. Apparently the Ironstone was not as popular as the company anticipated and was discontinued in 1972.

Known items made in Fiesta® Ironstone from a 1970s order form.

Cup/saucer
Mug coffee
Plate dinner 10"
Plate salad 7"
Bowl fruit dessert
Bowl soup/cereal
Bowl vegetable
Bowl salad 10 1/4"★
Platter oval 13"
Sugar covered
Cream
Sauceboat
Sauceboat stand
Salt shaker
Pepper shaker
Casserole covered★
Tea server covered★
Jug water 2 qt.★
Coffee server covered★
★These items sold only in Antique Gold according to a 1970 sales sheet.

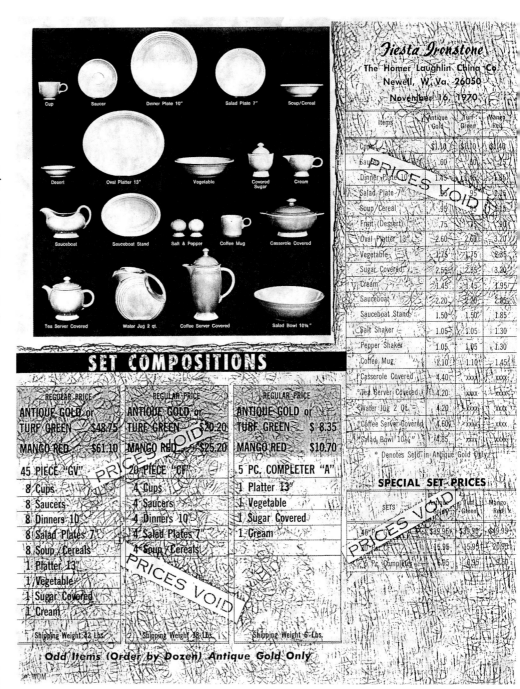

Fiesta Ironstone
The Homer Laughlin China Co
Newell, W. Va. 26050
November 16, 1970

Items	Antique Gold	Turf Green	Mango Red
Cup	1.10	1.10	1.40
Saucer	.60	.60	.75
Dinner Plate 10"	1.45	1.45	1.85
Salad Plate 7"	.95	.95	1.15
Soup/Cereal	.95	.95	1.15
Fruit (Dessert)	.75	.75	.90
Oval Platter 13"	2.60	2.60	3.20
Vegetable	1.75	1.75	2.35
Sugar Covered	2.55	2.55	3.20
Cream	1.45	1.45	1.95
Sauceboat	2.20	2.20	2.85
Sauceboat Stand	1.50	1.50	1.85
Salt Shaker	1.05	1.05	1.30
Pepper Shaker	1.05	1.05	1.30
Coffee Mug	1.10	1.10	1.45
Casserole Covered	4.40	xxxx	xxxx
Tea Server Covered	4.20	xxxx	xxxx
Water Jug 2 Qt.	4.20	xxxx	xxxx
Coffee Server Covered	4.60	xxxx	xxxx
Salad Bowl 10¼"	4.85	xxxx	xxxx

* Denotes Sold in Antique Gold Only

SPECIAL SET PRICES

SETS	Antique Gold	Turf Green	Mango Red
45	39.96	39.96	49.95
CF	15.95	15.95	20.95
5 Pc. Completer	6.95	6.95	

PRICES VOID

SET COMPOSITIONS

REGULAR PRICE
ANTIQUE GOLD or
TURF GREEN $48.75
MANGO RED $61.10
45 PIECE "GV"
8 Cups
8 Saucers
8 Dinners 10
8 Salad Plates 7
8 Soup/Cereals
1 Platter 13
1 Vegetable
1 Sugar Covered
1 Cream
Shipping Weight 42 Lbs.

REGULAR PRICE
ANTIQUE GOLD or
TURF GREEN $20.20
MANGO RED $25.20
20 PIECE "CF"
4 Cups
4 Saucers
4 Dinners 10
4 Salad Plates 7
4 Soup/Cereals
Shipping Weight 18 Lbs.

REGULAR PRICE
ANTIQUE GOLD or
TURF GREEN $ 8.35
MANGO RED $10.70
5 PC. COMPLETER "A"
1 Platter 13"
1 Vegetable
1 Sugar Covered
1 Cream
Shipping Weight 6 Lbs.

PRICES VOID

Odd Items (Order by Dozen) Antique Gold Only

Homer Laughlin advertising sheet (November 16, 1970) showing Fiesta Ironstone.

Fortune

The Fortune shape is a short set comprised of a cup, saucer, small plate, fruit and cereal bowl. The cups have solid turquoise interiors. The Fortune shape was produced for Quaker Oats as a premium offer in boxes of cereal. This is one of those shared-production shapes and you will also find pieces marked Fortune, Taylor, Smith & Taylor.

Fortune shape decoration unknown saucer and cup. set $8-10

Genesee 1911

The Genesee shape was advertised as a being a new shape in the 1912 Homer Laughlin *China Book* catalog. Genesee has smooth rims and rounded handles. The body of the ware is rather plain. It can be found in undecorated white and many decorations typical of the day.

Known pieces made in the Genesee shape:
Row 1: Item 1- teapot, Item 2-sugar and cover, Item 3-cream, Item 4-sugar individual, Item 5-cream individual, Item 6-covered butter, Item 7-teacup/saucer, Item 8- coffee cup/saucer, Item 9- after dinner coffee cup/saucer
Row 2: Item 10- Nappy, Item 11-coupe soup, Item 12- oatmeal, Item 13-fruit, Item 14-butter individual, Item 15- one dish, Item 16-bowl deep, Item 17-eggcup, Item 18-spooner
Row 3: Item 19-platter, Item 20-cake plate, Item 21-plate, Item 22-baker, Item 23-celery tray, Item 24-dish pickle
Row 4: Item 25-sauce-gravy boat/stand, Item 26-sauce-gravy boat fast stand, Item 27-covered dish, Item 28-oyster tureen, Item 29-casserole, Item 30-sauce tureen complete, Item 31-jug

Genesee shape saucer and cup, Virginia decoration. $10-15 set

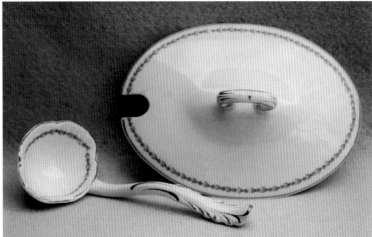

Ladle, decoration number G-254. $20-25
sauce tureen lid $20-25

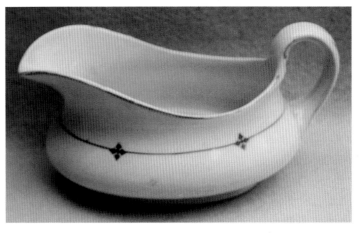

Genesee shape sauceboat, decoration number G-280. $15-20

Genesee shape plate, decoration number G-286. $10-12

Genesee shape plate, decoration number G-300. $10-12

Genesee shape covered vegetable dish, decoration number G-1405. $25-30

Genesee shape sauceboat, decoration number G-1601. $15-20

Page from a 1912 Homer Laughlin China book showing the G-1601 decoration.

Page from a 1912 Homer Laughlin China book showing the G-302 decoration.

Genesee shape saucer and cup, decoration number H-152. $15-20

Page from a 1912 Homer Laughlin China book showing the G-1703 decoration.

Genesee shape soup tureen lid, decoration number G1405. $15-18

Genesee shape covered dish, decoration number G-239. $25-30

Genesee shape covered dish, decoration number G-1101. $25-30

Genesee shape platter, Rose Spray decoration, luster edge. $15-20

Georgian Eggshell 1940

Georgian Eggshell was introduced in 1940 and was a lighter version of the Georgian Regular shape that was introduced in 1934. Georgian Eggshell was widely merchandised and many patterns can be found on this popular shape.

Known pieces made in the Georgian Eggshell shape: actual measurements

Tea cup	Bowl round vegetable
Saucer	Sauceboat
Plate 10"	Pickle
Plate square 8"	Sugar covered
Plate 6"	Cream
Bowl rim soup	Chop plate 14"
Bowl lug soup	Salt and Pepper
Bowl fruit 5"	Teapot covered 39 oz.
Platters 11", 13", 15"	Casserole covered
Bowl oval vegetable	

Genesee shape small jug, Yellow Rose decoration. $25-30

Genesee shape small jug, Red Rose decoration. $25-30

Georgian Eggshell shapes from Homer Laughlin China Company files.

Georgian Eggshell shape saucer/
cup set, Admiral decoration. $10-15

Georgian Eggshell shape plate, American Forget
Me Not decoration number G3381. $10-12

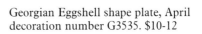

Georgian Eggshell shape plate, Arcadia (pink border) decoration
number G3527. $10-12

Georgian Eggshell shape plate, April
decoration number G3535. $10-12

Left:
Georgian Eggshell shape plate, Belmont
decoration number G3400. $10-12

Georgian Eggshell shape plate, Cardinal Variation decoration
number G3323. $10-12

Left:
Georgian Eggshell shape plate, Blue Chateau
decoration number G3468. $10-12

Georgian Eggshell shape teapot, Cashmere decoration number
G3391. $30-35

Left:
Georgian Eggshell shape plate, Bombay
decoration number G3461. $10-12

Georgian Eggshell shape plate, Chatham decoration number SR114. $10-12

Georgian Eggshell shape plate, Cotillion decoration number G3517. $10-12

Georgian Eggshell shape plate, Cosmos decoration. $10-12

Georgian Eggshell shape plate, Countess decoration number G3432. $10-12

Georgian Eggshell shape saucer/ cup set. Federal Pink decoration number G3348. $8-10

Georgian Eggshell shape plate, English Regency/American Mayflower decoration number G3357. $10-12

Right:
Georgian Eggshell shape, decoration number G3357. plates $10-12
cup $6-8
saucer $2-3
cream $10-12
sugar $10-15

Below:
Georgian Eggshell shape plate, Federal Blue decoration number G3353. $10-12

Georgian Eggshell shape luncheon plate, Fieldcrest also Kingston for Montgomery Wards, decoration number G3459. $10-15

Left:
Georgian Eggshell shape plate, Floral Medallion for Butler Brothers. $10-12

Georgian Eggshell shape plate, Marilyn Blue decoration number G3419. $10-12

Left:
Georgian Eggshell shape plate, Fruit Basket decoration. $10-12

Georgian Eggshell shape plate, Marilyn Pink decoration number G3418. The Marilyn Yellow decoration number is G3420. $10-12

Left:
Georgian Eggshell shape plate, Greenbriar decoration number G3499. $10-12

Georgian Eggshell shape bowl, Mexicana decoration. $15-18

Georgian Eggshell shape plate, Norway Rose decoration number CP202. $10-12

Right:
Georgian Eggshell shape cup, Pastel Tulip decoration. $8-10

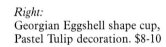

Georgian Eggshell shape plate, Moselle decoration number G3302. $10-12

Right:
Georgian Eggshell shape plate, Pink Chateau/ French Pink Chateau for Montgomery Wards decoration number G3467. $10-12

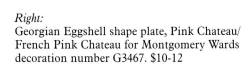

Georgian Eggshell shape plate, Rambler Rose decoration number VM2. $10-12

Georgian Eggshell shape plate, Rose Mary for Firestone Stores decoration number G3466. $10-12

Georgian Eggshell shape plate, Rhododendron decoration number G3436. $10-12

Georgian Eggshell shape saucer /cup set, Rosemont, Cynthia for Montgomery Wards decoration number G3351. $10-12

Georgian Eggshell shape plate, Sussex decoration number G3320. $10-12

Georgian Eggshell shape plate, decoration number G3324. $10-12

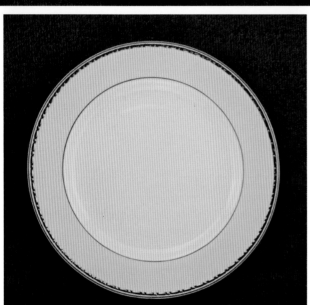

Georgian Eggshell shape plate, Viceroy for Montgomery Wards, American Empire decoration number G3330. $10-12

Georgian Eggshell shape plate, decoration number G3325. $10-12

Georgian Eggshell shape plate, decoration number G3323. $10-12

Georgian Eggshell shape plate, decoration number G3356. $10-12

Georgian Eggshell shape plate, decoration number G3380. $10-12

Georgian Eggshell shape, decoration number G3364. plate $10-12
cup $4-6

Georgian Eggshell shape plate, decoration number G3383.
Decoration number W450 for Woolworth. $10-12

Left:
Georgian Eggshell shape platter,
decoration number G3443. $15-20

Georgian Eggshell shape plate,
decoration number G3516. $10-12

Georgian Eggshell shape plate, decoration number G3466. $10-12

Left:
Georgian Eggshell
shape small plate, gold
edge trim and gold line,
decoration number
G3486. $4-6

Right:
Georgian Eggshell
shape plate, decoration
number G3527. $10-12

Georgian Regular 1934

The Georgian Regular shape was introduced and distributed both under the Craftsman trademark and the Georgian backstamp. The Craftsman line was developed for the better department stores and china shops.

Known pieces made in Georgian Regular: actual measurements
Plate dinner 10"
Plate luncheon 9"
Plate salad 8"
Plate dessert 7"
Plate bread and butter 6"
Plate rim soup 7 3/4"
Bowl fruit 5"
Bowl oatmeal 6"
Platter oval 11 1/2"
Platter oval 13 1/2"
Platter oval 15 1/2"
Bowl oval vegetable 9 1/2"
Round vegetable dish 9 3/4"
Round vegetable dish 8 3/4"

Tea cup and saucer
Cream soup cups and stands
Sugar covered
Cream
Casserole, covered
Gravy boat stand attached
Gravy boat
Pickle dish
Plate cake
Bowl round

Georgian Regular shape advertisement showing Carnelian decoration number G10.

Georgian Regular shape advertisement showing Chartreuse decoration number G9.

Georgian Regular shape cream, Formal decoration number G58. $10-15

Georgian Regular shape plate, Roselane decoration. $10-12

Georgian Regular shape plate, Gobelin decoration number G6. $10-12

Georgian Regular shape plate, decoration number G235. $10-12

Georgian Regular shape cup/saucer set, decoration number G168. $10-12

Golden Gate 1898

The Golden Gate shape was a pre-1900s shape and introduced possibly as early as 1896. As were most of the early shapes it was available in undecorated white and white with decorations. There were different shaped pieces used to make up the Golden Gate set composition.

Known Golden Gate pieces: trade measurements

A.D. coffee
A.D. saucer
Bakers 3", 6", 7", 8", 9"
Dish bone
Plate cake
Coffee cup/saucer
Dish covered 7", 8"
Casserole covered 7", 8"
Comportier
Cream
Cream individual
Custard
Dish (platters) 4", 7", 8", 9", 10", 11", 12", 13", 14", 16"
Egg cup
Bowl fruits 4", 5"
Jugs 6s, 12s, 24s, 30s, 36s, 42s
Jug Geisha 1s, 2s, 3s, 4s, 5s
Salad Newport 7", 8", 9"
Nut dish
Bowl oatmeal
Tureen oyster
Olive dish
Pickle
Plates 4", 5", 6", 7", 8"
Plate deep 7"
Plate coupe
Salad
Sauceboat
Tureen and stand
Sauce tureen and stand
Fancy slaw 7", 8", 9"
Soup tureen, stand and ladle
Spooner
Sugar and Geisha sugar
Sugar individual
Toast rack
Tea cup/ saucer
Teapot and Geisha teapot
Teapot individual

Golden Gate shapes from an early Homer Laughlin China Company catalog.

Golden Gate shapes from an early Homer Laughlin China Company Catalog.

Golden Gate shape cup and saucer set, Victorian Rose and Primula decoration. $15-18 set

Golden Gate olive dish, decoration number G102. $20-25

Golden Gate shape covered casserole, decoration number 412. $30-35

Granada 1967

Vincent Broomhall designed the Granada shape in 1967. The Granada shape is easily recognized by the half-circles around the outer rims.

Known Granada pieces: actual measurements
Buffet platter/chop plate
Cereal/soup bowl
Cream
Coffee server
Cup/saucer
Plate dinner 10"
Sugar covered
Salt and Pepper shaker set
Bowl vegetable

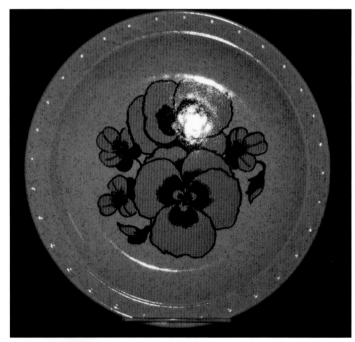

Granada shape plate, Fashion Flower decoration number SR-119. $6-8

DAYBREAK SR-128

■ for use in both microwave and conventional ovens
■ dishwasher safe ■ stores in refrigerator and freezer
■ glaze-sealed pattern for baked-in permanence

fashion house by NEWCOR T.M.

Made in U.S.A.
Newcor, Inc.
Wilmette, Illinois
60091

Granada shape, Daybreak decoration number SR-128.

Handy-Andy 1930s & 1940s

The Handy-Andy Specialty Company, Incorporated was located on Long Island, New York. The Handy-Andy Specialty Company dealt in juice extractors, vacuum bottles, metal lunch kits, revolving trays, chrome ware, china-ware, house wares and other specialties. The Homer Laughlin Company made casserole bowls to fit Handy-Andy's chrome ware frames. At least one other pottery company, Paden City Pottery, made bowls for the Handy-Andy frames.

There is no way to know all of the decorations of the Homer Laughlin Handy-Andy pieces but in 1938 the Murphy Company purchased 6 dozen HAS-15 casserole bowls; The May Company purchased 6 dozen HAS-14 bowls and several companies ordered number HAS-25. The HAS-25 casserole has an undecorated body and the lid was decorated in the Mexicana decoration. This is unusual as most Handy-Andy casseroles that we have seen have chrome lids.

Handy Andy covered OvenServe dish, metal frame and lid, orange-colored flower decoration. $30-35 complete set

Harlequin 1936

Harlequin was designed by Frederick Rhead and produced in 1936 but was not introduced until 1938. This colorful ware was made especially for the F.W. Woolworth stores. Harlequin was reissued in 1979 at the request of the F. W. Woolworth Company for their 100th anniversary.
Original Harlequin colors: Yellow, Green, Red, Blue
1940s colors: Tangerine (orange- red), Rose, Turquoise, Light Green
1950s colors: Gray, Chartreuse, Forest Green
1979s colors: Yellow, Turquoise, Medium Green, Coral

Known pieces made in the Harlequin shape: actual sizes

Tea cup/saucer	Tumbler
A.D. cup/saucer	Jug
Sauceboat	Ball Jug
Salt and Pepper	Nappy 9" round serving
Plate 10"	bowl
Plate 9"	Bowl oval vegetable
Plate 7"	Bowl cream soup
Plate 6"	Creamer high lip
Plate deep soup 8"	Creamer regular
Bowl fruit 5 1/8"	Sugar
Bowl 36s	Marmalade
Platters 10",13"	Candleholders
Tray relish, turquoise base	Casserole covered
with four pie shaped in-	Ashtray basket weave, regu-
serts	lar and saucer
Teapot	Egg cups double and single

Hanover 1950s

The Hanover Fine China Company, Incorporated purchased large amounts of Homer Laughlin China in the 1950s. They also had a line marked "Hanover" that utilized the Charm House shape of hollowware.

Charm House shape cream marked Hanover House. $10-14

HARLEQUIN W-336

16 PIECE STARTER SET

Left:
Harlequin shapes, number W-336 from a Homer Laughlin advertising sheet. W-336 is the number for the Rainbow colors or mixed color sets. The W stands for Woolworths. Harlequin Green is number W-337, Harlequin Coral is number W-338, Harlequin Turquoise is number W339 and Harlequin Yellow is number W-340.

HARLEQUIN — OPEN STOCK

The Homer Laughlin China Co.
NEWELL, WEST VIRGINIA

Copy of original paper print for Harlequin brochure.

Yellow Harlequin teapot covered casserole, covered sugar.

Harlequin shape, top row, left to right: yellow
teapot $80-85
blue double egg cup $15-20
green service pitcher $90-100
Middle row, left to right: yellow casserole $85-90
green 10" plate
$10-15
blue saucer $1-2
Front row, left to right: turquoise creamer $14-16
Rose salt/pepper in holder $35-40
yellow sugar with cover $18-20
rose jug $40-45
green fruit bowl $8-10

Green Harlequin Service Jug $90-100
Blue Novelty cream $20-25

1979 Harlequin Ironstone
dinnerware advertisement.

Harlequin / Tablefair 1980s

In the 1980s the Harlequin shape dinner plates, salad plates, and chop plates were combined with a hollowware shape called Tablefair. Since the older Harlequin had the Woolworth's letter W and a number, the letter W was combined with the letter T for Tablefair and became the Harlequin/Tablefair line. These late Harlequin colors were white and an "oatmeal like" color. There probably are more decorations but these are all that we were able to positively identify:

WT-100 Harlequin White
WT-101 Mayfair
WT-102 Suzanne
WT-103 Bounty

Harlequin shape ironstone, Strawberry decoration plate $8-10
International shape cup $3-4

Harlequin plates, experimental colors. No price established

Harlequin shape plate, Suzanne decoration number WT 102. $8-10
Tablefair shape cup $3-4

Late 1970s-1980s Oatmeal color Harlequin plate, cup, saucer. The Harlequin plates were used with many different shapes of hollowware. plates only $8-10

Harmony House

Harmony House was a brand name belonging to the Sears Roebuck and Company. Harmony House was used on dinnerware and many other items that were sold through the Sears Company stores and catalogs.

Harmony Sets Late 1930s

The Harmony sets, called Fiesta® Foursome, are combined sets of the Fiesta® ware and the Nautilus shape. "The Nautilus items are decorated with patterns which harmonize with the Fiesta® color selected for that particular set." The decorated Nautilus items are from the regular line and are numbers N-258 to go with yellow Fiesta®, N-259 to go with green Fiesta®, N-260 to go with red Fiesta®, and N-261 to go with the blue Fiesta®.

The correct combination of Fiesta® and Nautilus in the Harmony Sets: actual measurements
Nautilus
Eight 7" plates
Eight 4" plates
Eight tea cups
Eight 4" fruits
One 10" dish (platter)
One 7" baker
One 7" nappy

Fiesta®
Eight 10" plates
Eight 7" plates
Eight 6" desserts (soup/cereals)
One 15" chop plate
One 12" comport
Two bulb candlesticks
One salt and one pepper
One sugar and cover
One cream

Copy of a Homer Laughlin Company advertisement for the Fiesta Foursome Ensemble. The Fiesta Foursome Ensemble has previously been called Harmony Sets. The Red Fiesta® was sold with the Nautilus shape decoration number N260, the yellow Fiesta® with Nautilus shape decoration number N258, blue Fiesta® was paired up with Nautilus shape decoration number N261 and the green was sold with Nautilus shape decoration number N311.

Harvest

see Quaker Oats

Harvest decoration made for Quaker Oats. small plate $4-6 cup $4-6

Hearthside 1970s

The Hearthside shape was designed by Vincent Broomhall, art director of the Homer Laughlin China Company from 1963 until 1973. Hearthside's handles sit at an angle on the hollowware pieces and has ridges towards the base of the hollowware and on the rims of the flatware pieces.

Known Hearthside pieces: actual measurements
Buffet platter/ chop plate
Cream
Cup/saucer
Plate dinner 10"
Dish fruit
Salt and Pepper shaker set
Sugar covered
Bowl vegetable

Historical American Subjects

see Liberty

Hotel Ware 1900s

Most all of the potteries produced a white hotel ware line. Hotel ware lines were composed of necessary and useful items and the shapes used by the different potteries were very similar if not identical.

Homer Laughlin China Company advertising sheet showing Hearthside shapes with the Aztec, Petals, Delightful, Solitaire, Daybreak and Wheat decorations.

LAUGHLIN SEMI-VITREOUS HOTEL WARES, DOUBLE THICK.

dividual Cream, Seattle	8 Box Sugar	15 Coffee Mug, Baltimore	22 St. Denis Coffee	29 Plate	36 Baker, 3 inch
dividual Cream, Rocaille	9 Individual Cream, D. L.	16 Culot Coffee, Unhandled	23 St. Denis Tea	30 Globs Nappie	37 Covered Chamber
dividual Cream, Plain Oval	10 Individual Cream, B. H.	17 Culot Coffee, Handled	24 Seattle Coffee	31 Oyster Nappie	38 Burley Chamber
stard, Unhandled	11 Individual Cream, Tankard	18 Tulip Tea	25 Fast Drainer Butter	32 Oyster Bowl, Low Foot	39 Hall Boy Jug
stard, Handled	12 Individual Cream Saxon, Unhandled	19 Saxon Coffee	26 Ice Tub	33 Oyster Bowl, Footed	40 Rocaille Jug, 12s
und Restaurant Sugar	13 Individual Cream, Saxon, Handled	20 Saxon Tea	27 Dish, Oval	34 Ice Cream	41 Ice Jug
und Hotel Sugar	14 Coffee Mug, Straight	21 St. Denis After Dinner Coffee	28 Dish, Sterling	35 Individual Butter	42 Ewer and Basin

Page Thirteen

Shapes of Hotel ware from early Homer Laughlin catalog.

Left: round hotel sugar, Flower border. $20-25
round restaurant sugar, plain white undecorated (lid missing). $15-20

Household Institute 1941

The Household Institute line is made up of the Nautilus, Republic, Ovenserve and Kitchen Kraft shapes. The Household Institute line was the result of a 1941 agreement between The Homer Laughlin China Company and the Club Aluminum Company. The line was purchased specifically for Club Aluminum's continuity plans in their food stores divisions and was produced for several years.

Household Institute, all Priscilla decoration. Republic shape saucer and cup set $10-12
Republic shape plate $8-10
Kitchen Kraft jug $30-35

Household Institute Kitchen Kraft pie plate $25-30
cake plate $$20-25

Household Institute Kitchen Kraft open jug, Rhythm Rose decoration. $25-30

Hudson 1908

The Hudson shape was introduced in 1908 and was another popular pattern for The Homer Laughlin China Company. Hudson seems to be one of the easier early patterns for collectors to find. It can be found in plain white, gold trim, and a wide variety of decorations. The backstamp Majestic was applied on the Hudson shape and was sold to Butler Brothers. Majestic is not a shape name, but a line name.

Trade measurements

Row 1: Item 1-teapot, Item 2-sugar 30s, Item 3- cream, Item 4- individual sugar, Item 5- individual cream, Item 6- sauce boat, Item 7- bowl 30s, Item 8-coffee cup/saucer, Item 9-teacup/saucer, Item 10 -After Dinner coffee

Row 2: Item 11- salad 7", Item 12 -nappy 7", Item 13 -baker 7", Item 14- oatmeal 30s, Item 15- fruit 4", Item 16 -individual butter, Item 17- bone , Item 18 -pickle, Item 19- spooner

Row 3: Item 20- dish 10", Item 21- cake plate, Item 22- covered butter, Item 23- deep plate 7", Item 24- plate 7", Item 25- coupe soup 7"

Row 4: Item 26- oyster tureen, Item 27- covered dish 7", Item 28 -casserole 7", Item 29- sauce tureen complete, Item 30- celery tray, Item 31- jug 24s

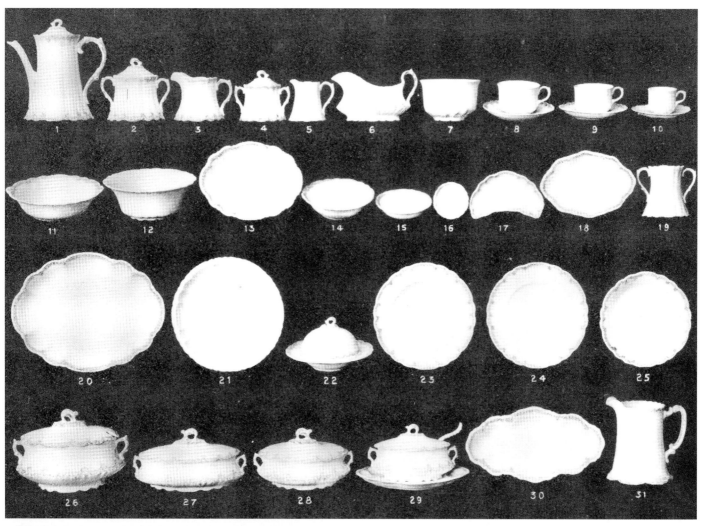

Hudson shapes from an early Homer Laughlin China Company catalog.

Hudson shape, Carnation Beauty decoration number SR25. plate $10-14
sauceboat $10-15

Hudson shape casserole, Carnation Beauty decoration number SR25. $75-95

Hudson shape sauceboat, Minton Rose decoration. $10-15

Hudson shape covered casserole, Peerless for Butler Brothers, Snowflake for Sears and Roebuck. $30-35

Hudson shape covered casserole, decoration number H41. $30-35

Hudson shape sauceboats, left decoration H3804, right decoration number H106. $10-15 each

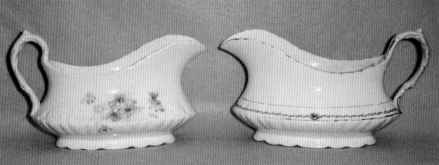

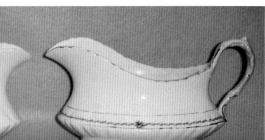

Hudson shape spooner, decoration number H60. $40-45

Hudson shape, decoration number H94. teapot $30-35 Graham cups $8-10 each

Hudson shape, decoration number H111. sauceboat $10-15
small Hudson plate $6-8

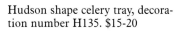

Hudson shape celery tray, decoration number H135. $15-20

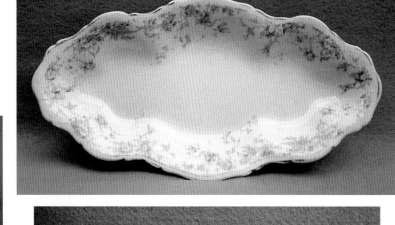

Hudson shape covered casserole, decoration number H111.
$30-35

Hudson shape cream, decoration number F.E.F. $10-15
right: small Hudson milk pitcher, decoration number H1104. $10-15

Hudson shape plates, left decoration number H129, right
decoration number H230. $10-12 each

Hudson shape covered sugar,
decoration number H1900. $10-15

Hudson shape plates: left gold stamp decoration for Butler Brothers, right decoration number H1699. $10-12 each

Hudson shape covered casserole, decoration number H94. $30-35

Hudson shape plates, left decoration number H2400, right decoration number H160. $10-12 each

Hudson shape covered casserole, decoration number H135. $30-35

Hudson shape plates, left decoration number H2500, right decoration number W 9 S. $10-12 each

Hudson shape covered casserole, decoration number 6704B. $30-35

Hudson shape covered casserole, decoration number H240. $30-35

Hudson shape covered casserole, decoration number H106. $30-35

Hudson shape covered casserole marked Majestic, decoration number H1107. Majestic is a name used for a line sold to Butler Brothers. The shape is Hudson. $30-35

Hudson shape covered casserole, "Mini Rose Border" decoration number H-36. $30-35

Hudson shape soup tureen, decoration number H87. $40-45

Hudson shape plate, decoration number H88. $10-12

International 1970s

The International shape was designed by Dennis Newbury. International is described as raised circles on the edge of the plates, saucers, bowls and platters. The colored glazes were the most popular. Decorations used on International were realistic flowers with simple bands of color on the outer rim.

Known items made in the International shape:

Dinner plate	Bread and butter plate
Salad plate	Dessert/fruit dish
Cup/saucer	Covered butter
Cereal/soup	Utility bowl
Covered casserole	Vegetable bowl
Beverage server	Round platter
Covered sugar	
Creamer	
Coffee mug	
Large coup soup	
Gravy boat	
Soup mug (like coffee cup but larger)	
Salt and Pepper	

International shape Ironstone dinnerware Sonata Brown decoration number IN-160.

International shape, Splendor decoration number IU-139. plate $4-6 saucer $.75-1.00
Unibody cup $2-3

International D.S. Company

The International D.S. Company was part of the Cunningham and Pickett organization of Alliance, Ohio.

Ivora 1938

The Ivora shape was introduced in 1938 and was a favorite with the Colgate Company as premium offers. The Ivora shape hollowware consists of two sizes of jugs. A covered sugar and cream was designed to go with the Brittany and Kwaker shape flatware.

International shapes from Homer Laughlin China Company files. Called Simplicity (solid white) when sold to Fashion House.

Ivora shape, pearlized finish with gold trim made for Quaker Oats. sugar $10-15
jug $35-40
cream $10-15

Ivory Color 1929

This shape was originally designed for use by the Sebring Pottery Company as their Barbara Jane shape. The Homer Laughlin China Company used it as a short set consisting of a cup, saucer, fruit bowl, cereal bowl and a small plate. The Quaker Oats Company ordered thousands of sets of Ivory Color to include in each box of Mother's Oats, or it could be ordered through the Quaker Oats catalogs.

Ivory Color small bowl $3-4.

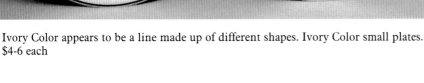

Ivory Color appears to be a line made up of different shapes. Ivory Color small plates. $4-6 each

Mother's Oats advertisement showing the Barbara Jane shape. Pieces made by the Homer Laughlin China Co with an L under the Ivory color mark.

Jade 1932

Frederick Rhead designed the Jade shape in 1932. Jade was dipped in a vellum glaze which is a soft ivory glaze, and also in a Clair de Lune glaze which is described as having the hue of moonlight. A 1933 spring issue of a Sears Roebuck catalog lists a 32- piece set of Jade for $7.95.

Known pieces made in Jade: trade measurements

Baker 9"
Baker 9 7/8"
Bowl 36s
Covered butter oblong
Cake plate 10 1/2"
Casserole 7 5/8"
Coffee cup
Saucer
Coffee, A.D. cup
Saucer
Cream 9 oz.
Cream soup and stand
Dish (platter) 11 1/2"
Dish (platter) 13 1/4"
Dish (platter) 15 1/8"
Fruit 5 3/8"
Jug 24s - 2 1/2 pints, covered and uncovered
Jug 42s - 3/4 pint
Nappy-7 1/2"
Nappy-9 5/8"
Nappy-8 3/8"
Bowl oatmeal 36s - 6 1/4"
Pickle 8 3/4"
Plate 6 1/8"
Plate 7 1/8"

Plate 8"
Plate 9"
Plate 9 7/8"
Plate 8 1/8"
Plate 6" deep flat soup
Sauce boat 6 3/4"
Sauce boat stand 5 3/8"
Sugar 9 oz. 30s
Cup
Saucer
Teapot 2 pints

Jade shape, decoration number J109. platter $30-35
saucer $3-4
open sugar $10-15

Jade shape plates, decoration numbers, left to right, Orange and blue flowers J105, Large pink and blue blossom decoration number J106, orange floral and leaf border decoration number J116. $10-15 each

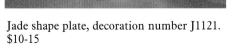

Jade shape plate, decoration number J1121. $10-15

Jade shape covered casserole, decoration Flowers of the Dell. $35-40

Jade shape plates, left to right, decoration numbers J207, J209, J212. $10-15 each.

Jade shape cup and saucer set, decoration number J9. $15-20

Jade shape dinner plate, decoration same as W5923. $15-18

Juanitaware late 1930s

Juanitaware is a term used to describe the ensembles that included colored glaze Riviera, glassware and colorful cutlery. The Homer Laughlin China Company did not provide the glassware or cutlery.

Juanitaware Ensemble featuring Riviera dinnerware in Azure Blue, Mission Yellow, Manzanita Red and Pampas Green. The ensemble including glassware and colored stainless steel cutlery was offered free with Norge Home Appliances.

Jubilee 1948

The Jubilee shape was designed by Don Schreckengost and was made to commemorate Homer Laughlin's 75th anniversary. (1873-1948). It was introduced at the 1948 Pittsburgh Dinnerware Show in solid colors of Celedon Green, Shell Pink, Mist Grey and Cream/Foam Beige. A 6 piece "Smart Starter Set" consisting of a 10" plate, 7" plate, 6" plate, 5 1/2" fruit, cup and saucer was offered for $3.10 per set. The Design Patent Serial No. 552,243 was filed on March 18, 1948.

Known items made in the Jubilee shape: Actual measurements

Teapot and cover

Tea cup/saucer
Coffee pot covered
A.D. coffee cup/ saucer
Egg cup double
Salt and Pepper
Platter 11"
Platter 13"
Chop plate 15"
Plate 10"
Plate 9"
Plate 7"
Plate 6"
Fruit 5 1/2"
Cereal soup 6"
Coupe soup (flat) 8"
Nappy 8 1/2"
Casserole covered

Jubilee shapes from a Homer Laughlin China Company brochure.

Below:
Jubilee shapes from a Homer Laughlin China Company brochure showing Celedon Green, Shell Pink, Mist Gray, Cream Beige.

SMART SET

Order these 6 piece Smart Sets as a basis of your Jubilee service. Then add to your set from the items listed below. Choice of four colors.
Price per Smart Set..................$2.75

OCTOBER 1, 1948

PRICE LIST
(PER PIECE)

ITEMS	Beige Gray Green Pink	ITEMS	Beige Gray Green Pink
TEA CUPS	.55	CHOP PLATES, 15"	1.95
TEA SAUCERS	.25	SUGARS, COV'D	1.35
PLATES, 10"	.75	CREAMS	.85
PLATES, 9"	.65	CASSEROLES, COV'D	2.50
PLATES, 7"	.50	SAUCEBOAT, FAS'T STAND	2.50
PLATES, 6"	.40	TEA POTS, COV'D	2.25
COUPE SOUPS, 8"	.65	COFFEE POTS, COV'D	3.25
FRUITS, 5½"	.30	COFFEE CUPS, A. D.	.50
CEREAL SOUPS, 6"	.45	COFFEE SAUCERS, A. D.	.25
NAPPIES, 8½"	.85	SALTS	.55
PLATTERS, 11"	1.10	PEPPERS	.55
PLATTERS, 13"	1.60	EGG CUPS	.60

DELIGHTFUL Color SELECTION

Celedon Green

Shell Pink

Mist Gray

Jubilee's sophisticated shape and colors offer a charming compliment to any decorative motif. Light in weight, Jubilee is elegant for dinner, luncheon, breakfast, buffet; for any service, any occasion.

Cream Beige

© 1948 The Homer Laughlin China Company
Newell, W. Va.

PRESENTING a Jubilee DINNERWARE

Karol China – Karolyte

Karol China is another one of the multitude of companies who purchased Homer Laughlin china and marketed it under their own brand name.

Rhythm shape plate, gold decoration marked "Karol China, Regalyte". Warranted 22 Kt. Gold. $10-15

Kenilworth 1955

Kenilworth is a small "buffet-luncheon-snack" set designed by Don Schreckengost for a metals manufacturer who had plants in both New Jersey and New York. Kenilworth was produced in solid glazes of white, pink, turquoise and black. The earliest pieces of Kenilworth have decals copied from actual poker chips provided by the customer and are rare. Metal lids, handles and frames for Kenilworth were provided for and put together by the customer. There may be other Kenilworth pieces and there may be pieces marked Kenilworth that were not made by the Homer Laughlin China Company.

Known items made in the Kenilworth shape: actual measurements

Salad bowl 10 3/8" x 3 1/2" deep
Shrimp bowl 11 3/8" x 2 7/8" deep
Cereal bowl 5 1/2" x 2" deep
Casserole body 8 1/4" x 3 1/2"
Coffee bottle 6 3/8" x 10 3/16" tall
Coffee pot
Sugar body
Cream
Platter oval, 15"
Platter/large round
Ice bucket
Casserole large covered 10 3/4"
Casserole small covered
Ash tray fluted
Lazy Susan two styles

Note: A small bowl used with Kenilworth is the Rhythm shape, Charm House shakers and coffee cups were used with Kenilworth. One order shows that Epicure plates were sold to go with the Kenilworth shape.

Kenilworth shape number 301 coffee bottles with a variety of metal tops. Complete with lids and metal handles. $100-125 each

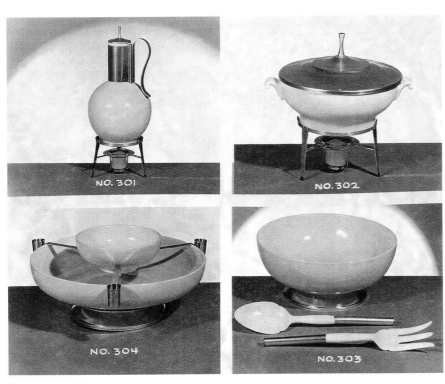

Kenilworth shapes: Number 301 coffee bottle if complete $100-125
Number 302 salad bowl with metal lid and frame $75-80
Number 304 chip and dip set complete $125-150
Number 303 salad bowl with salad fork and spoon $50-75

Kenilworth shape jug, Casino poker chip decorations. No price established

Kenilworth shape number 302 turquoise salad bowl, metal lid and frame $75-80

A variety of Kenilworth shape pieces from a collection. No price established

Kingsway

The Kingsway China Company is believed to be part of the Cunningham and Pickett organization of Alliance, Ohio. It is possible that it is a line made for Cunningham and Pickett.

King Charles 1905

The King Charles shape is a very ornate, vintage dinnerware dating back to the early 1900s. A 1905 Fall and Winter Sears Roebuck catalog offered an 80 piece set of the Arbutus White and Gold pattern for $7.99. The same pattern could be ordered in four different size sets as well as open stock.

Known pieces made in King Charles (not a complete list): trade measurements

A.D. coffee cup	Soup coupe
A.D. saucer	Cream
Baker	Plate deep
Bone dish	Dish fruit
Bowl oatmeal	Jug
Butter covered	Mustard
Butter individual	Nappy
Casserole covered	Tureen oyster
Pot chocolate	Tureen soup
Cup chocolate	Spooner
Cup coffee	Sugar covered
Saucer coffee	Tea cup/saucer
Compote	Teapot

Kings Charles shapes from a 1903 Homer Laughlin China Company catalog.

King Charles shape chocolate pot, Lily & Wild Pinks turquoise air brush trim. *Not marked Art China.* $75-100

King Charles shape platter, Garland Wreath decoration. $20-25

King Charles shape chocolate pot Portrait Pitcher, *Not marked Art China.* $100-115

King Charles shape handled pickle dish, Lily & Wild Pinks with gold trim. *Not marked Art China.* $20-25

King Quality 1950s

King Quality is just one of the many names used by companies who purchased Homer Laughlin China ware under their own company name or their own brand name.

Kitchen Kraft 1937

Kitchen Kraft was introduced at the Merchandise Mart, Chicago Glass and Pottery Market on August 2nd, 1937. Kitchen Kraft was advertised as a sturdy, durable new graceful shape calculated to appeal to discriminating purchasers. Dipped in Fiesta® colors of red, yellow, light green, cobalt and ivory also ivory with attractive decorations. The Kitchen Kraft patent number 399,815 was filed on November 15,1937.

Known items made in Kitchen Kraft: actual measurements
Cake server
Cake plate 10"
Pie plate 9 1/2"
Covered jars-small, medium, large
Covered casserole 8 1/2"
Individual casserole 7 1/2"
Serving spoon
Serving fork
Mixing bowls 10", 8", 6"
Refrigerator set-3 piece stacking set with one lid
Plates, two sizes 6", 9"

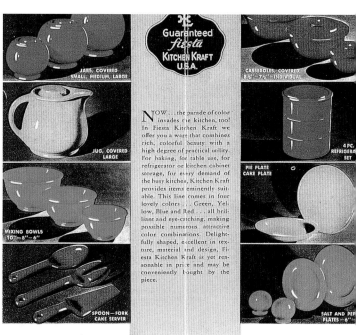

Kitchen Kraft shapes from a Homer Laughlin China Company brochure.

Kitchen Kraft shape mixing bowl, Petit Point decoration. $25-30

Kitchen Kraft shape pie plate, Chinese Porcelain decoration. $25-30

Kitchen Kraft shape pie plate, China Lady decoration. $25-30

Kitchen Kraft shape covered casserole, Chinese Princess decoration. $25-30

Kitchen Kraft shape medium bowl, Chinese Porcelain decoration. $25-30

Kitchen Kraft shape pie plate, Chinese Three decoration. $25-30

Kitchen Kraft shape pie plate, Kitchen Bouquet decoration. $25-30

Kitchen Kraft shape pie plate, Rhythm Rose decoration. $20-25

Kitchen Kraft covered jug, Spring Wreath decoration number C-A-C186. $30-35

Kitchen Kraft jug, Priscilla decoration number K351. $25-30

Kitchen Kraft shape pie plate, Silhouette decoration number C-A-C55. $20-25

Kitchen Kraft shape covered jars left, Starflower decoration. $65-75 right, Mexicana decoration number KK324. $100-125

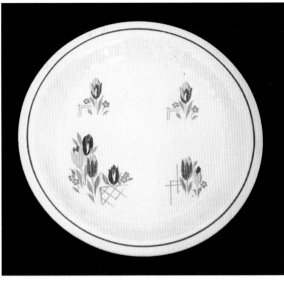

Kitchen Kraft pie plate, decoration number K303. $30-35

Kitchen Kraft mixing bowl, Sun Porch decoration. $75-95

Kitchen Kraft pie plate, Willow variant decoration. $30-35

Kraft Blue and Kraft Pink 1937

The Kraft line was made in both soft blue and soft pink. It has a delicate thin body with an embossed rope-like outer rim with white handles and white knobs on the hollowware. A few hand-painted pieces have been found on Kraft Blue.

The following items were produced in the Kraft Pink W-241 line and the Kraft Blue W-337: trade measurements

Tea cup/saucer	Sugar, covered
Cream soup	Teapot/cover 31 oz.
Double egg cup	Novelty cream
Oatmeal 36s	Kraft Blue (W-337)Same as
Nappy 7"	Kraft Pink with the follow-
Fruit 4"	ing additions:
Plate 4"	Plate deep soup 6"
Plate 5"	Baker 7"
Plate 7"	
Dish (platter) 8"	
Dish (platter)10"	Kraft shapes from Homer
Cream	Laughlin files.

KRAFT BLUE — OPEN STOCK

Kraft shapes, left, Kraft Pink cream
$10-12
covered sugar $12-14
plate $8-10
right, Kraft Blue eggcup $10-12
cream soup $14-16
plate, large $10-12

Kraft Blue cream, Marcia decoration. $10-15

Kraft Blue, decoration number GC M10l. covered
sugar $10-15
cream $10-15

Kwaker 1924

Kwaker flatware is plain and undistinguished, but the hollow-ware has distinctive square handles and knobs. The Kwaker shape was very popular with both the Butler Brothers and Sears Roebuck Company. A 1926 Sears catalog lists a 100 piece set of the Garland pattern for $27.95 with $5.00 down and $4.00 a month payment.

Known pieces made in Kwaker: trade measurements

Row 1: Item l-sugar, Item 2-cream, Item 3-teapot, Item 4-After Dinner cup/saucer, Item 5-bouillon cup and saucer, Item 6-teacup/saucer, Item 7-coffee/saucer, Item 8-bowl 36s

Row 2: Item 9-fruit 4", Item 10-oatmeal 36s, Item 11-covered butter, Item 12-fast stand sauce boat, Item 14-coupe soup 7", Item 15-nappy 7"

Row 3: Item 16-platter 12", Item 17-cake plate, Item 18-plate 7", Item 19-pickle dish, Item 20-baker 7"

Row 4: Item 21-handled salad, Item 22-casserole dish 7", Item 23-covered salad, Item 24-covered dish 7", Item 25-jug 24s

Kwaker shapes from a Homer Laughlin China Company catalog.

Kwaker shape sauceboat, Neville decoration number K2253. $10-15

From the morgue; Kwaker plate, decoration number K-2713. No price established

Kwaker shape, Presidential decoration for Butler Brothers. open casserole $20-25
small platter $15-20
large platter $20-25

From the morgue; Kwaker shape plates, left decoration number K-7103, right K-3623, No price established

Kwaker shape plate, Rose and Ivory decoration for Sears and Roebuck. $10-12

Kwaker gravy liner/pickle dish, gold Fleur-de-lis decoration number K-5501. $12-15

Kwaker shape plates left, decoration number K1027, right decoration number K8677M. $12-14 each

Left:
Kwaker shape pitcher, decoration number K2413. $15-20

Kwaker shape plate, decoration number K4ll5. $12-14

Kwaker shape, decoration number K6115. small plate $8-10 cream and covered sugar set $25-30

Kwaker shape plate, gold and floral decoration number K3115. $12-14

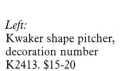

Enlargement of K6115 decoration.

Kwaker shape plates, left decoration number K7077M, right decoration number K8177M. $12-14 each

Kwaker shape plates, left decoration number K7877 and right decoration number K3377. $12-14 each

Kwaker shape plates, left decoration number K8077, right decoration number K6877. $12-14 each

Kwaker shape plates, left decoration number K8477, right decoration number JJ647. $12-14 each

Right:
Kwaker shape plates, left decoration number K8723, right decoration number K5913. Plates each $12-14.

Below:
Kwaker shape covered sugar, decoration number K7017M. $15-20

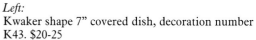

Kwaker shape covered dish, decoration number K647. $20-25

Left:
Kwaker shape 7" covered dish, decoration number K43. $20-25

Right:
Kwaker shape covered dish, decoration number K1523. $20-25

Kwaker shape covered dish, decoration number K4502. $20-25

Kwaker shape platter, decoration number K1815. $20-25

Right:
Kwaker shapes, Rosewood decoration, called Caledonia when sold to Sears and Roebuck Company. covered casserole $30-35
platter $20-25
sauce boat $10-15
covered sugar $10-15
cream $10-15

Below:
Kwaker shapes, decorated with Golden Fleece decoration
cream $20-25
teapot $40-45
covered sugar $10-15

Below left:
Kwaker shape jug, Three Roses decoration with orange to rust trim. $35-40

Below:
Kwaker shape, made for the East Liverpool Chamber of Commerce. covered sugar $10-15
cup/saucer set $10-15
cream $10-15
platter $20-25

Lady Greenbriar and Lady Stratford

Lady Stratford and Lady Greenbriar mixed shape sets from a 1950s Homer Laughlin China Company catalog.

Nautilus shape plate, Lady Greenbriar decoration. $15-18

Nautilus shape, Lady Stratford teapot $50-75
Lady Greenbriar teapot $50-60

Nautilus shape plate, Lady Stratford decoration. $15-20

Laughlin International 1961

The Laughlin International was a 1961 agreement between the Homer Laughlin China Company and the International China Company of the Cunningham and Pickett organization, thus the name Laughlin International. The Homer Laughlin Company manufactured all of the chinaware sold by Laughlin International. They also retained approval of the products to be sold through the sales organization of Laughlin International.

Liberty 1942

Liberty was possibly the last shape Mr. Rhead helped develop before his death in November of 1942. The Liberty shape is described as having a gadroon edge, which is a type of fluting around the edge. Liberty is a medium weight ware with a traditional shape. It was reported as not being well received by buyers, but was produced for nearly 10 years.

Known pieces made in the Liberty shape: trade measurements
Tea cup/saucer

Plate 8"	Dish (platter) 12"
Plate 7"	Dish (platter) 10"
Plate 6"	Dish (platter) 8"
Plate 5"	Casserole, covered
Plate 4"	Sugar covered
Deep plate (soup)	Cream
Fruit 4"	Sauceboat regular
Oatmeal 36s	Pickle
Baker 7"	Teapot and cover
Nappy 7"	Bowl 36s Empress shape

Liberty shape small plate, Blue Heaven decoration number AS6. $4-6

Back, Liberty shape plate, Calirose decoration number CP86. $8-10
Front, Liberty shape covered sugar and cream set, Magnolia decoration number L623. $20-25

Liberty shapes from Homer Laughlin Company advertising.

Liberty shape plate, Colonial Kitchen also known as Colonial Fireplace, decoration number L608. $8-10

Liberty shape cup/saucer set, Colonial Kitchen/Colonial Fireplace decoration. Gold trim. $10-12

Liberty shape plate, Greenbriar decoration number CP96. $8-10

Liberty shape small plate, Dogwood decoration number L613. $4-6

Liberty shape cream, Petit Point decoration. $8-10

Liberty shape plate, Dolly Madison decoration. $6-8

Liberty shape plate, decoration number L615. $8-10

Liberty shape platter, Spring Wreath
decoration CAC186. $20-25

Liberty shape, Queen Esther decoration. cream $10-15
covered sugar $10-15
plate $10-12

Liberty shape, Pastel Tulip decoration. platter $20-25
cream $10-12
sugar $12-14

Liberty shape plate, Lattice Rose decoration. $10-12

Liberty shape plate, Magnolia decoration. $8-10

Liberty shape plate, "Autumn Leaves" decoration. $10-12

Historical American Subjects 1940-1941

The Historical American Subjects decoration is one of the more popular patterns in the Liberty shape. It was made for Woolworth's in blue- number W-449 and in pink- number W-342. The scenes on the Historical American Subjects were reproduced from original engravings by Joseph Boggs Beale.

Listed are decorations used on individual pieces: trade measurements

Tea cup/saucer	Franklin's experiment
	The Mayflower
Plate 4"	Paul Revere
Plate 5"	Liberty Bell
Plate 6"	Purchase of Manhattan Island
Plate 7"	Betsy Ross and flag
Plate 8"	George Washington takes command
Plate deep 6"	Ponce De Leon discovers Florida
Bowl fruit 4"	Lincoln-Rail splitter
Bowl oatmeal	Stagecoach
Bowl nappy	Pony Express
Baker 7"	Lincoln's Gettysburg Address
Dish (platter) 8"	Clermont
Dish (platter) 10"	First Thanksgiving
Cream	Star Spangled Banner
Sugar covered	Barbara Ritchie
Casserole covered	Border print
Tea pot covered	Paul Revere

Liberty shape plates, Historical America decoration. Left, 8" salad plate, Purchase of Manhattan Island. $10-12
right, 7" salad plate Liberty Bell decoration. $8-10

Liberty shape 13" platter, Historical America decoration, First Thanksgiving. $20-25

Liberty shape casserole and cover, "Open Rose" decoration. $25-30

Lifetime China

The Lifetime Company was part of the Cunningham and Pickett organization based in Alliance, Ohio.

Louis XVI 1891

The Louis XVI shape is an elegant style of embossed scrolls around the rim with tusk like handles. This shape was the first to use the name Laughlin beneath the Lion and Eagle backstamp. A set was exhibited at the 1893 Columbian Exposition in Chicago. Decorators used a beautiful technique of adding matte color shadows around the edges, and the handles were treated in a color of burnt ivory. The Patent Design number 20,968 for Louis XVI was dated July 28, 1891.

Known Louis XVI pieces: trade measurements
Butter individual
Casserole covered
Cream
Jug
Plate 10"
Platters 13", 15"
Sauceboat
Sugar covered

Left:
Louis XVI shape jug with gold air brush over lemon yellow body. $100-125

Louis XVI shape jug with pastel flowers with gold scroll work. $100-125

Majestic Early 1900s

Majestic is not a shape name, but a line of dinnerware made by The Homer Laughlin China Company and sold to Butler Brothers. Hudson seems to be the shape of choice for the Butler Brothers Company, but other Homer Laughlin shapes may have been used for the Majestic line.

Marigold-1934

Frederick Rhead designed the Marigold shape. The main features of the Marigold shape are the small-embossed fan like designs spaced around the rims. It is sometimes referred to as a cousin to the Virginia Rose shape. Since the Virginia Rose was such a popular shape, Marigold lost its sales appeal, and was dropped after a few years of production. 1941 orders show solid green glazed Marigold sold to the G.C. Murphy Company.

Known pieces made in the Marigold shape: trade measurements

Tea cup/saucer	Nappies 6", 7", 8"
Bakers 6", 7", 8"	Oatmeal 36s
Bowl 36s	Plate 4", 5"
Dish 7", 8"	Square plate 6"
Double egg cups	Plate 7", 8"
W.W. egg cups (Woolworth)	Deep plate 6"
Fruit bowl 4"	Bowl coupe 7"
Fruit bowl 5"	Sugar
Jug 42s	
Cream	

Marigold shape cup/saucer, Pennsylvania Dutch decoration. $8-10 set right, small plate, decoration number M211. $4-6

Marigold shape, Springtime decoration number W245. small plate $4-6
cream $10-12

Marigold shape platter, Mexicali decoration. $25-30

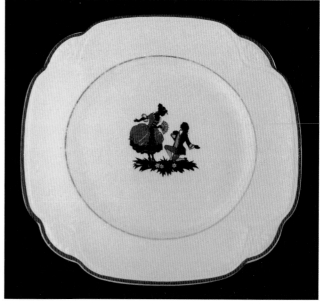

Marigold shape plate, Silhouette decoration number CAC55. $8-10

Marigold shape plates; left green trim decoration number M90, right red trim decoration number M110. $8-10 each

Marigold shape plate, decoration number M207. $8-10

Marigold shape casserole and cover, Spring Flowers decoration number M156. $32-38

Marigold shape platter, Mexicana decoration. $20-25

Marigold shape plate, decoration number same as G3515. $8-10

Marigold shape plate, Mexicana decoration. $12-14

Marigold shape plate, Petit Point decoration for Cunningham and Pickett. $6-8

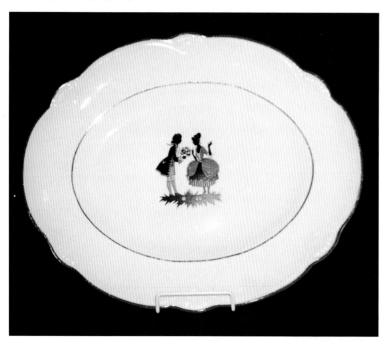

Marigold shape platter, Silhouette decoration. $15-20

Marigold shape plate, Rhododendron decoration. $8-10

Marigold shape, solid green glaze. flat soup $10-12
small plate $6-8

Modern Farmer-1938

The original Modern Farmer shape was produced at the James River Pottery at Hopewell, Virginia and was introduced in 1938 with a decoration called Riviera. Homer Laughlin completed producing the shape and continued to use the name Modern Farmer although it was first referred to in art department notes as "Hopewell". Some of the shapes were redesigned for Homer Laughlin's automatic jigger equipment. There did not seem to be a demand for this unusual shape and it was dropped after a short production run.

Known pieces made in Modern Farmer: actual measurements

Tea cup/saucer	Creamer
Plate bread and butter 6"	Vegetable dish covered
Plate salad/pie 7"	Vegetable dish round open
Plate 9"	Vegetable dish oval open
Plate dinner 9 3/4"	Gravy boat
Plate (flat soup) 7 1/2"	Gravy boat stand
Cream soup	Platter 11"
Sauce dish 5 1/4"	Platter 13"
Sugar and cover	Platter 15"

Modern Farmer shape cups, the cup on the left is made by Homer Laughlin China Company and is the Breton decoration number MF2. The cup on the right was made by the James River Pottery. $8-10 each

Modern Farmer shape, Petit Point decoration. $10-12

Modern Farmer shape, Gascon decoration number MF3. left plate $8-10 small bowl $4-6

Modern Farmer shape, Breton decoration number MF2. shakers $14-18 set
open sugar $8-10
cream $8-10
saucer $2-3
cup $8-10

Modern Farmer shape, Scattered Daisies decoration. sauceboat $15-20
liner $8-10

Left:
Modern Farmer shape plate, Mexicana decoration. $14-16

Modern Farmer shape plate, Nova Flower decoration
number MF13. $8-10

Modern Farmer shape Scattered Daisies sauceboat $15-20
liner $8-10
covered sugar $14-16
cream $8-10
Modern Farmer cake set, Gold'n Flowers decoration. $45-50

Modern Star 1958

Rhythm shape, Modern Star decoration number Q22.
small plate $4-6
cup $4-6

Modern Star is not a shape but a short dinnerware set with undistinguishing characteristics. The Taylor, Smith and Taylor Pottery also made the Modern Star pattern for the Quaker Oats company. The Homer Laughlin Company shared production with T.S.&T. on several of the Quaker Oats orders.

Known items made with Modern Star decoration: actual measurements	Additional Modern Star items that could be ordered by the customer:	
Tea cup/saucer	Platter 8"	actual size 11"
Plate 4"	Platter 10	actual size 13"
Bowl fruit	Nappie 7"	actual size 8 1/2"
Bowl oatmeal	Plate 7"	actual size 9 1/4"
	Plate 8"	actual size 10 1/4"

Nautilus Eggshell 1937

Nautilus Eggshell was the first Eggshell shape and was introduced in 1937. The Nautilus Eggshell shape is a traditional plain shape, very light weight with formal and informal decorations. The edges are thin and delicate and the texture is rich and uniform to emulate fine china.

Known pieces made in Nautilus Eggshell: actual measurements
Dinner plate 10"
Breakfast plate 9
Large salad plate 8"
Pie or salad plate 7"
Bread and butter plate 6"
Square salad plate
Platter (oval)11"
Platter (oval)15"
Round Chop platter 14"
Sauce/fruit dish
Pint bowl 5"
Sauceboat stand/pickle 9"
Gravy with attached stand 9"
Tea cup/tea saucer
Rim/coupe soup 8"
Gravy boat
Lug/onion "ear-ed" soup
Cereal/oatmeal bowl
Handled cream soup 6"
Round open vegetable bowl 8 1/2"
Oval open vegetable bowl 8 3/4"
Covered vegetable 10"
Cream pitcher
Covered sugar

Nautilus Eggshell shape plate, decoration number N1576. $10-12

Nautilus Eggshell shape plate, Orchard decoration number N1773. $10-12

Nautilus Eggshell shape, Nantucket decoration also called Penthouse. saucer $2-3
cup $6-8
plate $10-12

Nautilus Eggshell shape plates, left decoration number N1525, right decoration number N1481. $10-12 each.

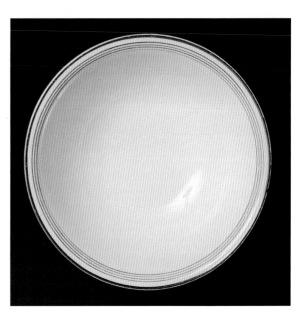

Nautilus Eggshell small bowl, Empress decoration number N1219 Platinum trim lines, four narrow lines and one wider line around the edge. $4-6

Nautilus Eggshell shape. Pastel Tulip decoration when sold to Jones, McDuffie, Strater in 1941, called Sublime when sold to Seller Lowengart in 1946, called Tulip Garland and Marianne when sold to Hibbard, Spencer and Bartlett in 1950. Pastel Tulip seems to be the favorite name with collectors. cream $10-12
covered sugar $14-16
cup $6-8
saucer $2-3

Nautilus Eggshell bowl, outside platinum trim, two wider platinum lines and three narrow lines towards the inside of the bowl, decoration number N1539 made for the Pearl China Company. $8-10

Nautilus Eggshell oval vegetable bowl, Acacia decoration number N1410. $12-15

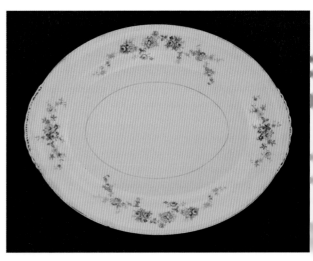

Nautilus Eggshell shape platter, Annette decoration number N1705. $15-20

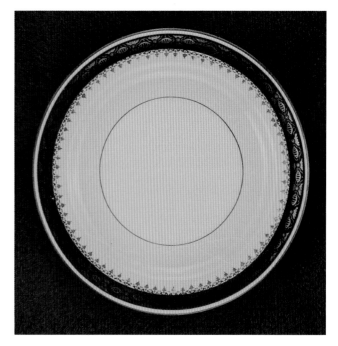

Left:
Nautilus Eggshell shape square salad plate, Admiral decoration number N1708. $12-15

Nautilus Eggshell shape plate, Calais decoration number N1578. $10-12

Nautilus Eggshell shape plate, Ardmore decoration number N1583 also called Marlborough. $10-12

Nautilus Eggshell shape plate, Cardinal decoration number N1653 also called Grandeur. $10-12

Nautilus Eggshell shape plate, Blue Dawn decoration number N1691. $10-12

Right:
Nautilus Eggshell shape plate, Dresden decoration
made for Cunningham and Pickett. $10-12

Nautilus Eggshell shape plate, Calirose decoration number
N1580. $10-12

Nautilus Eggshell shape plate, Dubarry decoration number
N1802. $10-12

Nautilus Eggshell shape plate, Daisy Field decoration
number N1510. $10-12

Nautilus Eggshell shape plate, Garland decoration
number N1590 also called Dubarry. $10-12

Left:
Nautilus Eggshell shape plate, Gardenia decoration number VM101. $10-12

Nautilus Eggshell shape plate, Magnolia decoration number N1775. $10-12

Nautilus Eggshell shape plate, Gold Dawn decoration number N1483. $10-12

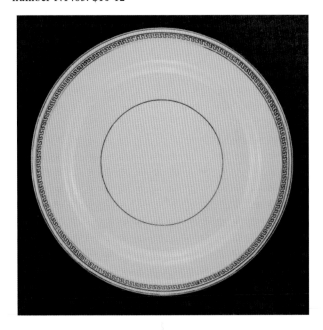

Nautilus Eggshell shape plate, Magnolia decoration, gray band N1776. $10-12

Nautilus Eggshell shape plate, Greek Key also called Grecian Key decoration number N1694. $10-12

Nautilus Eggshell shape platter, Starflower
decoration number N1471. $15-20

Nautilus Eggshell shape plate, Moss Rose decoration
number N1627 also called Apple Blossom. $10-12

Nautilus Eggshell shape square salad plate, Talisman
decoration number N1750. $12-15

Nautilus Eggshell shape plate, Pink Petal decoration
number N1769. $10-12

Nautilus Eggshell shape plate, White
Rose decoration number N1781. $10-12

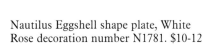

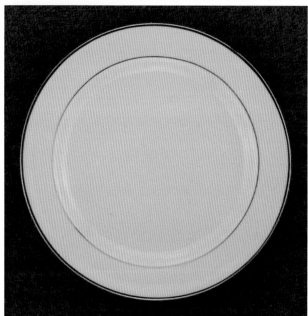

Nautilus Eggshell shape plate,
decoration number N1223. $10-12

Nautilus Eggshell shape plate, decoration number N1746.
$10-12

Nautilus Eggshell shape plate, decoration number N1730.
$10-12

Nautilus Eggshell shape plate, Countess decoration.
$10-12

Nautilus Eggshell shape plate, decoration number N1732
also called Three Feathers by collectors. $10-12

Nautilus Eggshell shape plate, Aristocrat decoration. $10-12

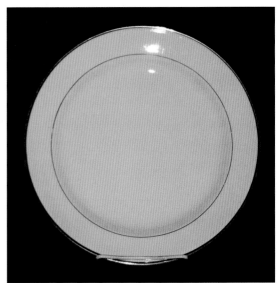

Nautilus Eggshell shape plate, Cherry Blossom decoration number N-1670. $10-12

Nautilus Eggshell shape plate, Petit Point decoration number N-1458. $10-12

Nautilus Eggshell shape plate, gold trim decoration number N-1652. $10-12

Nautilus Eggshell shape sugar without lid, decoration number N1637. $8-10. With lid, $14-16

Nautilus Regular 1936

This shape proved to be the most popular of all shown at the 1936 Summer House and Furnishing Show. Two characteristics of this shape are the distinctive four feet on the hollowware and the shell shape knobs.

Known pieces made in the Nautilus Regular shape: trade measurements

A.D. cup	Nappies 7", 8"
A.D. saucer	Bowl oatmeal
Bakers 7", 8"	Onion soup
Bowl 36s	(lugged oatmeal)
Casserole covered	Pickle dish 6"
Soup coupe 7"	Plates 4", 5", 6", 7", 8"
Cream	Plate deep 6"
Dish (platters) 8", 10", 12"	Sauceboat regular
Double egg cup (Cable	Sugar covered
shape)	Tea cup/saucer
Bowl fruit 4"	Teapot

Nautilus Regular shape plate, Hacienda decoration. $12-15

Nautilus Regular shape cream, Colonial decoration number CP53. $10-14

Nautilus Regular shape cream, Magnolia decoration number CP145. $10-14

Nautilus Regular shape plate, decoration number N388. $10-12

Nautilus Regular shape plate, Old Curiosity/Antique Shop decoration number W138. $8-10

Nautilus Regular shape covered sugar and cream, Red Apple decoration. $20-25 set

Nautilus Regular shape platter, Arizona decoration number N1406. $15-20

Below:
Nautilus Regular shape plate, Petit Point/Heirloom decoration number N1332.

Nautilus Regular shape, Red Line decoration number W-238. covered sugar $10-14
sauceboat $10-15
liner $8-10

Nautilus Regular shape sauceboat with solid green glaze. $15-20

Nautilus Regular shape cup and saucer,
decoration number N-205. $10-15 set

Newell 1928

The Newell shape was introduced in 1928. From an old ad: "The tendency toward graceful lines and delicate modeling promises to be a feature of the popular taste for 1928." It was the first shape designed by newly employed art director, Frederick Rhead. Mr. Rhead wrote in his journal: December 26. 1927 "photograph of Newell shape for catalogs". The Newell shape replaced Hudson in the 1929 Homer Laughlin catalogs. The Newell Patent Design Serial Number 27,575 was filed on July 25,1928.

Row 1: Item 1-coffee cup/saucer, Item 2-sugar/cover, Item 3- casserole covered, Item 4-cream, Item 5- tea cup/saucer
Row 2: Item 6- bowl 36s, Item 7- teapot, Item 8- sauce/gravy boat, Item 9- A.D. cup/saucer
Row 3: Item 10- nappy 7", Item 11- platter 10"(old measurements), Item 12- pickle dish
Row 4: Item 13- bouillon cup/saucer, Item 14- cake plate, Item 15- covered butter, Item 16- plate 7", Item 17- coupe soup-7"
Row 5: Item 18-fruit 4", Item 19-fast stand sauce boat, Item 20-jug 24s, Item 21-sauce boat/pickle dish/liner, Item 22-oatmeal bowl

Newell shapes from a 1926 Homer Laughlin China Company catalog.

Newell shape small pitcher, Blue Bird
decoration. $20-25

From the morgue; Newell shape plates,
left decoration number N-7128, right N-
7715. No price established

From the morgue; Newell shape plates,
left decoration number N-2123, right N-
2723. No price established

From the morgue; Newell shape plates,
left decoration number N-2228, right N-
2628. No price established

From the morgue, Newell shape plates, left decoration number N-5728, right N-8228. No price established

From the morgue; Newell shape plates, left decoration number N-5628, right N-2728. No price established

From the morgue; Newell shape plates, left decoration number N-3628, right W-429-30. No price established

From the morgue; Newell shape plates, left decoration number N-7100, right N-3023. No price established

From the morgue; Newell shape plates, left decoration number N-3923, right N-7415. No price established

Left:
Newell shape cup and saucer, Poppy decoration. $12-15 set

Right:
Newell shape bowl, decoration number N75 called Southern Pride for Butler Brothers also called Song of Spring for Sears Roebuck. $18-20

Newell shape casserole lid, decoration number N3028. $12-15

Newell shape plates decoration number N80 and N7415. $10-15 each

Newell shape plates decoration number N2723 and decoration number N3923. $10-15 each

Newell shape plates, decoration numbers N2124 and N5428. $10-15 each

Newell shape plates, decoration numbers N2823 and N5202. $10-15 each

Newell shape plates, decoration numbers N4143 and N3943. $10-15 each.

Newell shape plates, decoration numbers N7128 and N3928. $10-15

Newell shape covered sugar, decoration number N2023. $10-15

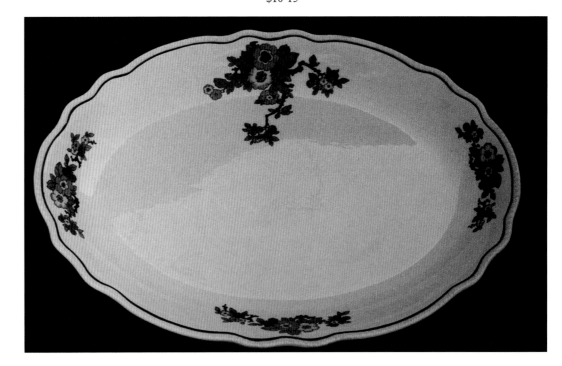

Newell shape platter 27 1/2"
decoration number N2023.
$25-30

Niagara 1910

The Niagara shape was introduced in 1910. Niagara is easily confused with the Genesee shape and the difference is ever so slight. One difference is that an incised line circles near the bottom of the hollowware. A 1910 Spring Sears and Roebuck catalog lists 60 pieces of Killarney on the Niagara shape for $10.95.

Row 1: Item 1-teapot, Item 2-sugar, Item 3-individual sugar, Item 4-cream, Item 5-covered butter, Item 6-tea cup/saucer, Item 7-coffee cup/saucer, Item 8-After Dinner coffee cup/saucer

Row 2: Item 9-nappy, Item 10-baker, Item 11-oatmeal, Item 12-fruit, Item 13-individual butter, Item 14-bone dish, Item 15-bowl, Item 16-Boston egg cup, Item 17-spooner

Row 3: Item 18-dish (platter), Item 19-cake plate, Item 20- plate, Item 21-coupe soup, and Item 22-pickle dish

Row 4: Item 23-sauce boat and stand, Item 24-sauceboat fast stand, Item 25-casserole, Item 26-covered dish, Item 27-sauce tureen complete, Item 28-jug

Niagara shape plate, decoration number N199. $8-10

Niagara shape sauceboat, Killarney decoration number N169. $10-15

Niagara shape plate, decoration number K16. $8-10

Niagara shape plate, decoration number N224. $8-10

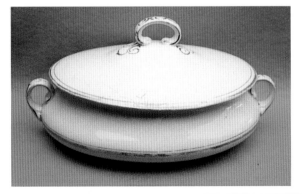

Left:
Niagara shape covered casserole, decoration number N192. $20-22

Right:
Niagara shape plate, decoration number N552. $8-10

Oak

See Introduction, Shapes

A SHAPE OF OLD ENGLISH STYLE PRODUCED TO MEET THE DEMAND FOR A PRACTICAL AND SENSIBLE TEA AND COFFEE . . . GRACEFUL BUT STURDY, OF LIBERAL CAPACITY, AND WITH A VARIETY OF DECORATIVE TREATMENTS, THE NEW OAK TEA AND COFFEE IS AN UNUSUALLY ATTRACTIVE LOW PRICED SPECIALTY.

Oak shape cup and saucer from a Homer Laughlin ad.

Old Roman 1928

This shape was first produced for Quaker Oats as a giveaway in boxes of cereal. It was sent to Quaker Oats on September 14, 1928 for their approval, and was given the okay for production on October 17, 1928. Old Roman was produced in solid colors of green or yellow as well as applied decorations. A 1934 Montgomery Wards catalog listed a 32- piece set of Snowflower pattern for $4.39.

Known items produced in the Old Roman shape: trade measurements

Baker 7"	Plate 7"
Cream	Plate deep 6"
Sugar open	Plate square 6"
Dish (platter) 8"	Tea cup/saucer
Fruit 4"	Bowl oatmeal
Plate 4"	

Roman Pheasant decoration on Old Roman shape.

Old Roman shape saucer and cup, Roman Pheasant decoration number K4415. $20-25 set

Old Roman shape, solid yellow baker. $35-40

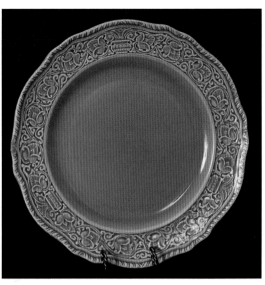

Old Roman shape plates decoration number OR47 and OR58. No price established on morgue items.

Old Roman shape plate, solid green glaze. $20-25

Old Roman shape plates, decoration numbers OR51, OR52, and OR53. No price established on morgue items.

Old Roman shape plates, decoration number OR65 and OR55. No price established on morgue items.

Old Roman shape vegetable bowl decoration number same as VR 316. $30-35

Old Roman shape flat soup, bowl with green band. $20-25

Old Roman shape, decoration number OR65. plate $15-20 plain undecorated cup $15-18

Orbit 1960s

Orbit is a 1960s hollowware shape used with Brittany flatware and/or Rhythm flat ware. The hollowware has white inside with the color on the outside. The plates are in white with a decoration the same color as the hollowware. Homer Laughlin art director, Vincent Broomhall designed the Orbit shape.

Known items produced in the Orbit shape: actual measurements

Tea cup, color outside	Hostess tray 12 1/2",
Tea saucer, decorated	decorated
Dinner plate 10", decorated	Sauceboat, color outside
Pie or salad plate 7",	Cream, color outside
decorated	Sugar covered, color outside
Bread and butter plate	Round vegetable dish
6", decorated	8 1/2", color inside
Cereal soup, color outside	Butter cover, colored body
Chowder soup, color inside	white
Fruit 5 1/2" dessert, color	Coffee server, color outside
inside	Salt, color outside
Platter 11 1/2", decorated	Pepper, color outside
Platter 13 1/2", decorated	

Orbit shape Vista decoration number RUS120

Orbit shape Trent decoration number B1474.

Orbit shape Orient decoration
number RUM 705.

Orbit shape Maplewood
decoration number B1473

Below:
Orbit shape plate, Maplewood
decoration number B1473. $6-8

Orbit shape teapot light pumpkin yellow with white lid. No price
established on morgue items

Orleans 1932

The Orleans shape was introduced in 1932. Orleans is another shape first produced as an exclusive for the Quaker Oats Company, then later released for sale to other companies. The shape features a rose embossed border and is somewhat like Ravenna in design.

Known items produced in the Orleans shape yellow glaze: actual measurements
Bakers 8 ¼", 9 ¼"
Bowl 36s
Dish (platters) 10 ½", 11 ½", 13"
Bowl fruit 5 5/8"

Nappies 7 7/8", 9"
Cream
Sugar open
Jugs 36s
Pickle 8 7/8"
Plates 6", 7", 8", 9", 10"
Plate deep 7", 8"
Sauceboat
Tea cup/saucer

In another list of the Orleans shape Ivory glaze there was no 8" baker listed. There was a 10" dish (platter) listed but no 6", a sauce boat and pickle dish were listed in the ivory glaze but not the yellow glaze. This does not mean that these items were not made in both glazes.

Orleans shape decoration O-20 from Homer Laughlin files. No price established

From the morgue; Orleans shape plates, left decoration number O10, right O16. No price established

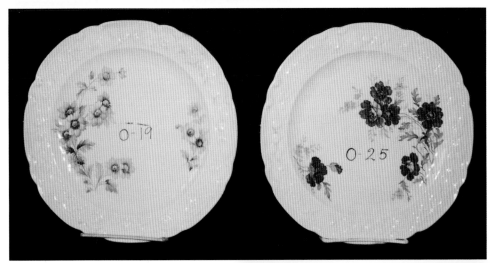

From the morgue; Orleans shape plates, left decoration number O19, right O25. No price established

From the morgue; Orleans shape plates, left decoration number O27, right O28. No price established

From the morgue; Orleans shape plates, left decoration number O31, right O32. No price established

From the morgue; Orleans shape plate, decoration number O34. No price established

From the morgue; Orleans shape plate, decoration number O35. No price established

From the morgue; Orleans shape plates, left decoration number O39, right O37. No price established

From the morgue; Orleans shape plates, left decoration number O65, right O63. No price established

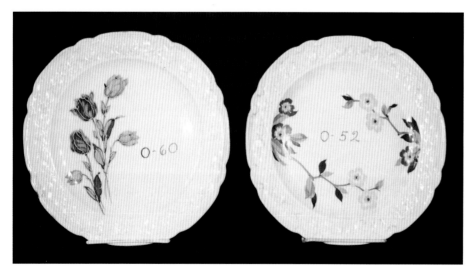

From the morgue; Orleans shape plates O60, right O52. No price established

From the morgue, Orleans shape oval vegetable bowl decoration number O79. No price established

From the morgue, Orleans shape cream, platinum trim decoration number O74. No price established

From the morgue, Orleans shape platter same decoration as Trellis T95 and Ravenna RV25. No price established

Orleans shape plates from the morgue O43 and O45. No price established

OvenServe 1933

OvenServe was introduced in 1933 and was designed by Frederick Rhead. It consists of a comprehensive series of shapes designed for baking, broiling, chilling, freezing and otherwise preparing food. Various sizes of casseroles, pie plates, dessert dishes and baking dishes were made in OvenServe. In order to provide a perfect table setting, cups, saucers and three sizes of serving plates were produced. OvenServe was made in Orange (called Pumpkin by collectors), Melon Yellow, Ivory and Ivory with decorations. Quaker Oats ordered such huge quantities of OvenServe, that the Homer Laughlin Company could not keep up and pieces such as ramekins and French casseroles were farmed out to Taylor, Smith and Taylor. It was a common practice for potteries to help each other out when they received very large orders. The OvenServe patent number 346,279 was filed July 31,1933. The numbers in the listing below were given by the company to identify the OvenServe pieces and were taken from an original OvenServe brochure.

Known items made in the Ovenserve line: actual measurements
Baked Apple Dish #502-5"
Baked Beans, Individual open #203-4"
Baking Dishes oval, #101-6", #102-8", #103-11"
Baking Dishes round, #104-4 1/2", #105-5 1/2", #106-
7", #107-8 1/2"
Bean Pots covered, #201-4 1/2", #202-5 1/2"
Bowls, Mixing 12", 11", 10", 9", 8"
Casseroles French open #304-4 1/2", #305-5 1/2"
Casseroles Round covered #301-6", #303-8 1/2", 10"(no number)
Coffee cups-#401, Saucers #402
Custards #501-3 1/2"
Pie Plates #601- 9"
Pie Plates 9 1/2" Daisy Chain
Pie Plates #602-10 1/2"
Pie Plates individual #600-5 1/2"
Plates #403-7", #404-9", #405-10"
Platter Fish #701-9 1/2"
Platters deep #702-11 1/2", # 703-13 1/2"
Pudding dish, #503-6"
Ramekins #504-3 3/4"
Shirred egg dish #801- 6"
Welsh Rarebits #802-7"
Sugars, open
Creams
Pie Knives/cake server
Salad spoon long
Salad spoon short
Covers for #302 round baking dish 5 1/2"
Jug

OvenServe shape small casserole, decoration number OS404. $8-10

OvenServe shape, decoration number OS54. covered casserole $20-25
underplate $10-12

OvenServe shape casserole, decoration number OS90. $20-25

OvenServe shape, decoration number OS65.
covered casserole $20-25
underplate $10-12

OvenServe shape underplate, decoration number OS88. $10-12

OvenServe shape pie plate, decoration number OS90. $20-25

OvenServe shape underplate, decoration number OS67. $10-12

OvenServe shape covered casserole,
decoration number OS111. $20-25

Pastoral

See Quaker Oats

Pastoral shape saucer and cup, Pastoral decoration. $6-8 set

Peachtree 1936

Peachtree was introduced in 1936 for the Quaker Oats Company as premium offers in boxes of cereal. The only known items in Peachtree are a cup and saucer. In September of 1937, 9,000 dozen cups and saucers were shipped to the Quaker Oats Company.

Peachtree shape saucer and cup. $6-8 set.

Pearl China 1931- present

The Pearl China Company was formed in 1931 by George and Dennis Singer as a pottery outlet. Their new store was opened in 1939 on Dresden Road in East Liverpool, Ohio and they distributed items from many companies including the Homer Laughlin China Company. Some items will be marked only Pearl China and some will be double stamped with both the Homer Laughlin and the Pearl China backstamps.

Perfection Early 1900

Perfection appears to be a Butler Brothers line that was supplied by several American potteries including the Homer Laughlin China Company.

Piccadilly 1940

The Piccadilly shape was introduced in 1940. It was modeled soon after Brittany and was first referred to as "New Brittany" but late in 1939 the name was changed to Piccadilly. It utilized the Brittany flatware.

Known pieces made in the Piccadilly shape:

Cream	Tea cup
Cream soup	Sugar
Sauceboat	Casserole covered

Piccadilly shape plate, decoration number P516. $8-10

Later Piccadilly shape, Mary Anne decoration. small plate $4-6
dinner plate $8-10
cup/saucer $8-10 set

Princeton 1936

The Princeton shape has embossed roses and leaves spaced around the rim and is trimmed in blue, maroon or light green. It is a short set of tea cups, saucers and dinner plates. It was first produced in 1936 for F.W. Woolworth but was later sold to other companies. A 1940 Bechtel, Lutz and Jost Spring catalog lists a dozen plates for $1.25.

Princeton shape plate. $4-6

Princeton shape cup. $2-4

Priscilla

See Household Institute

Quaker Oats

Harvest QO19
Pastoral QO20
Wild Rose QO21

All three patterns were produced as an exclusive premium for the Quaker Oats Company and was offered in boxes of their cereal. All three patterns were referred to as Pastoral ware by the Quaker Oats Company. All three patterns are the same shape. Wild Rose is the only pattern of the three that is known to have additional items which could be ordered from Quaker Oats by sending in coupons found in boxes of Quaker Oats cereal.

Known pieces:
Tea cup/saucer
Bowl small fruit
Bowl oatmeal
Plate small 5"

Other shapes ordered by Quaker Oats: Modern Star, Peachtree, Tea Rose, Doric, Ivory Color, Chelsea, Wells, Ravenna, Trellis, Carnival, Brittany, 3 piece child's set made up of a Purina bowl, Ovaltine mug and a 5" plate.

Mother's Oats China Brand advertisement from a February 1928 The Farmer's Wife magazine, showing the Barbara Jane shape made for Quakers Oats marked Ivory Color. If the piece was made by Homer Laughlin there will be an L under the Ivory Color mark. **See also Harvest, Pastoral, and Wild Rose**

Rainbow Ware

Rainbow Ware was a term used by the Homer Laughlin China Company in the late 1930s in reference to their Fiesta® ware line.

Ravenna 1932

Frederick Rhead designed the Ravenna shape which was introduced in 1932. The design is similar to the Orleans shape and the flatware is easily confused. However, the hollowware is different.

Known pieces in the Ravenna shape: actual measurements

Baker 9 1/4"	Bowl fruit 5 1/4"
Cream 1/2 pint	Nappy 8 1/4"
Sugar 30s open	Plates 10", 9"
Sugar covered	Plate 8 1/8" deep flat soup
Platter 11 1/8"	Sauceboat
Platter 13 1/4"	Tea cup/saucer

Ravenna shapes decoration number RV509.

Ravenna shape platter, Morning Side decoration. $20-25

From the morgue; Ravenna shape plates decoration number RV45 and RV1143. No price established

From the morgue; Ravenna shape plates, left decoration number RV12, right RV5. No price established

From the morgue; Ravenna shape plates, left decoration number RV7, right RV3. No price established

From the morgue; Ravenna shape plates, left decoration number RV20, right RV19. No price established

From the morgue; Ravenna shape plates, left decoration number RV23, right RV31. No price established

From the morgue; Ravenna shape plates, left decoration number RV28, right RV27. No price established

From the morgue; Ravenna shape plates, left decoration number RV47, right RV49. No price established

From the morgue; Ravenna shape plates, left decoration number RV1043, right RV34. No price established

Left:
From the morgue; Ravenna shape plate, decoration number RV9533. No price established

Right:
From the morgue; Ravenna shape plate, decoration number RV9233. No price established

From the morgue; Ravenna shape plate, decoration number RV36. No price established

From the morgue; Ravenna shape plate, no decoration number Flower Garland. No price established

Ravenna shape plates decoration number R48 and RV52. $8-10 each

From the morgue; Ravenna shape plate, decoration number RV50. No price established

Ravenna shape plates decoration number R8733 and R8333. $8-10 each

From the morgue; Ravenna shape plate, decoration number RV1343. No price established

Ravenna shape plate, same decoration as RV404. $8-10

Regency 1966

The Regency shape was designed by Vincent Broomhall, art director of The Homer Laughlin China Company. The Regency shape is made up of fine ridges on the hollowware and edges of the flatware.

Known Regency pieces: actual measurements

Cup	Platters 11", 13"
Saucer	Bowl vegetable
Plate dinner 10"	Cream
Plate salad 7"	Sugar covered
Plate bread and butter 6"	Coffee pot covered
Bowl fruit/dessert	Sauceboat
Bowl large soup 8"	

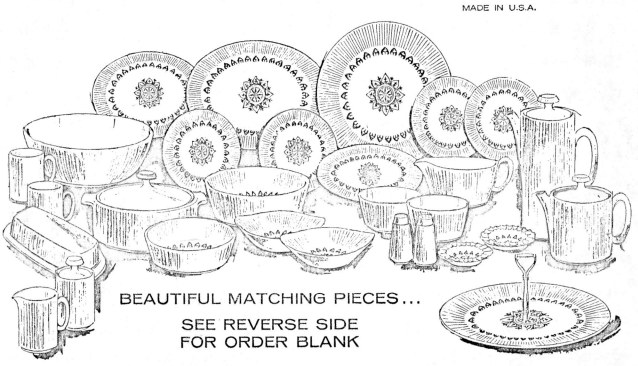

Regency shapes, Serenade dinnerware from Homer Laughlin China Company advertising sheet.

Regency shape, Serenade line
cup and saucer $6-8 set
fruit/cereal $4-5
large plate $6-8
small plate $2-3
cream $6-8

Republic 1916

This shape is considered "the grand old lady of Homer Laughlin shapes", as it was produced from 1916 through the 1960s. The Republic shape was a favorite with Sears Roebuck, although it was also sold by Alden's, Cunningham and Pickett, Butler Brothers, F.W. Woolworth and Montgomery Wards. A 1949 Wards catalog lists a 53- piece set of Republic for $17.95. A 1919 Sears catalog lists a 112 piece set for $22.92 which weighed 100 pounds. Most all of the potteries had a shape very similar to Republic.

Trade measurements

Row 1: Item 1-teapot, Item 2-sugar 30s, Item 3-cream, Item 4-individual sugar, Item 5-individual cream, Item 6-sauce boat, Item 7-sauce boat fast stand, Item 8-bowl 30s

Row 2: Item 9- coffee, Item 10- tea cup & saucer, Item 11- after dinner coffee, Item 12- nappy 7", Item 13- baker 7", Item 14- oatmeal 30s, Item 15- fruit 4", Item 16- individual butter, Item 17- bone dish

Row 3: Item 18-pickle dish, Item 19-dish (platter) 10", Item 20-cake plate, Item 21-covered butter, Item 22-deep plate 7", Item 23-plate 7"

Row 4: Item 24-coupe soup 7", Item 25-oyster tureen, Item 26-covered dish 7", Item 27-casserole 7", Item 28-sauce tureen complete, Item 29-jug 24s

THE HOMER LAUGHLIN CHINA COMPANY, NEWELL, W. VA.

THE REPUBLIC DINNER SERVICE.

1 Teapot	7 Sauce Boat, Fast Stand	13 Baker, 7 inch
2 Sugar, 30s	8 Bowl, 30s	14 Oatmeal, 30s
3 Cream	9 Coffee	15 Fruit, 4 inch
4 Individual Sugar	10 Tea	16 Individual Butter
5 Individual Cream	11 After Dinner Coffee	17 Bone Dish
6 Sauce Boat	12 Nappy, 7 inch	18 Pickle

19 Dish, 10 inch	25 Oyster Tureen
20 Cake Plate,	26 Covered Dish, 7 inch
21 Covered Butter	27 Casserole, 7 inch
22 Deep Plate, 7 inch	28 Sauce Tureen Complete
23 Plate, 7 inch	29 Jug, 24s
24 Coupe Soup, 7 inch	

Republic shapes from a Homer Laughlin China Company catalog.

Republic shape small plate, Apple Blossom decoration. $6-8

Republic shape small plate Blue Birds, decoration number R1726. $12-15

Republic shape small plate, Blue Willow decoration. $8-10

Republic shape plates, decoration numbers W114 and N4343. $10-12 each

Republic shape teapot (no lid) Priscilla decoration. $15-18
complete $25-30

Republic shape plates, decoration number R1804 called Calvert for Butler Brothers, decoration number R9524 Maple Leaf. $10-12 each

Republic shape plates, Rhododendron and Daisy Field decoration. $10-12 each

Republic shape cream, decoration number R9724. $12-15

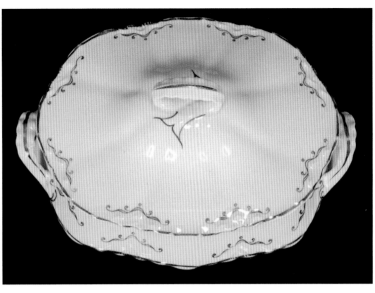

Republic shape soup bowl, decoration number R1104. $8-10

Republic shape covered dish, decoration number R5001. $25-30

Republic shape covered sugar, decoration number R5901. $14-18

Republic shape covered dish, Orchard decoration for Sears. $25-30

Republic shape, Wildflower decoration. cup/saucer $10-12 set
cream $12-15
covered sugar $14-18
plate $8-10

Republic shape, "Pastel Tulip" decoration. Back row platter $18-20, front row 9" plate $8-10, soup bowl $8-10, cup/saucer set $8-10, fruit bowl $5-8

Rhythm 1950

Rhythm was designed in 1950 by Don Schreckengost. It was advertised as "latest modern shape, beautiful lines. Available undecorated or decorated in a variety of smart new decorations and in four colored glazes, Harlequin yellow, burgundy, dark green and chartreuse." Gray was added soon after the original four colors.

Known items made in the Rhythm shape: actual measurements

Casserole covered	Platter 11 1/2", 13 1/2"
Bowl cereal/soup	Salt shaker
Bowl coupe soup 8"	Pepper shaker
Cream	Sauce boat
Sugar covered	Tea cup
Fruit 5 1/2"	Tea saucer
Nappy 9"	Tea pot covered
Pickle	Water jug
Plates 6", 7", 8", 9", 10"	

Rhythm shapes from a Homer Laughlin Company Rhythm brochure.

Rhythm shape plates, American Provincial decoration. $8-10 each

Rhythm shape cream, Autumn decoration number RY159. $8-10

Rhythm shape, London decoration number IU2. covered sugar $10-15
platter $10-15
White Flower decoration number RY252. sauceboat $8-10
small plate $4-6

Rhythm shape 6" plate, Colonial Kitchen decoration. $6-8

Rhythm shape plate, Madrid decoration. $8-10

Rhythm shape, Dubarry decoration number CP133.
covered sugar $10-15
cream $10-12
small plate $6-8

Rhythm shape, Rubaiyat decoration number RY263. plate $8-10
covered sugar $10-15
cream $10-12

Rhythm shapes from a Homer Laughlin advertising sheet showing Golden Wheat and Capri decorations.

Rhythm shape plate, Sweet Pea decoration number W350. $8-10

Rhythm shapes Western decoration made for Woolworth's decoration number W251. Cup and saucer $12-16 set, cereal bowl $12-16, fruit bowl $10-12, 9" plate $15-20

Rhythm shapes colored glazes. Teapot $45-55, 10" plate $10-15, cup and saucer set $10-15. Some Rhythm colors may command a higher price.

Rhythm shapes, Lotus Hai decoration number RY135. Called Silver Lotus when sold to the Bohnsack Company.

Rhythm shape, Allegro decoration also called Adrian when sold to the John Plain Company. $8-10

Rhythm shape bowl, Dubarry decoration. $10-12

Rhythm shapes, Capri decoration number RY172.

Rhythm shape platter, White Flower decoration number JJ152 for Newberry's. $12-16

Rhythm shapes Harvest Gold decoration for Cunningham and Pickett. 6" plate $5-7, cup $5-7, 10" plate $8-10

This lovely high-styled pattern—"As New As Tomorrow"—sets the fashion note in contemporary dinnerware design.
The delicate harlequin motif in crisp, fresh decorator-colors of turquoise, gray and black makes "FIFTH AVENUE" the first choice of the sophisticated hostess.

The Homer Laughlin China Co.
NEWELL,   WEST VIRGINIA

CROCKERY & GLASS JOURNAL for May, 195

Fifth Avenue decoration from a 1950's trade journal.

Rhythm shape bowl, Red Apple decoration number JJ150. $10-15

Riviera 1936

Riviera is a colored glazed ware on the Century shape. Riviera was glazed in Blue (called Mauve Blue by collectors), Yellow, Light Green, and Tangerine (orange red). Riviera was part of an ensemble called Juanita or Juanita ware by the Homer Laughlin China Company. The Juanita ensemble included glassware and cutlery. The four colors remained throughout the 1930s and a 1941 order still shows only the four original colors. In 1943 "Red went to war" and ivory was substituted for the Tangerine colored glaze. An October 1948 composition sheet continues to show the Blue, Yellow, Light Green and Ivory colors. The Homer Laughlin China Company only sold Riviera in four- mixed colors.

Known items made in the Riviera/Century shape: trade measurements

Dish (platters) 8", 10"	Sauceboat
Cream	Sauceboat fast stand
Deep plate (soup) 8"	Baker 8"
Fruits 4"	Jug covered
Mug handled	Teapot
Nappy 7"	Bowl oatmeal 6"
Plates 4", 5", 7", 8"	Butter rectangular
Sugar covered	Batter set three pieces: large
Teacup/saucer	covered jug, small open
Bowl 36s	syrup, rectangular tray
Salt and pepper set, Tango	Pitcher disc
shape	Tumbler

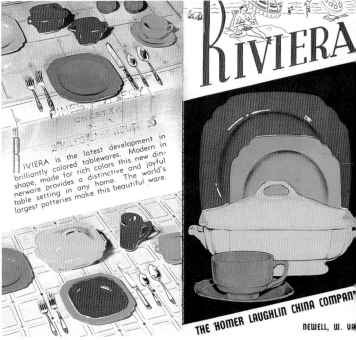

Homer Laughlin China Company Riviera brochure.

Riviera shapes from a Homer Laughlin Company Riviera brochure.

Large collection of colored Riviera ware

From the morgue, green Riviera console bowl. Riviera candleholders were also made to make up this centerpiece sample set. (not produced). No price established on morgue items.

Rococo 1891

In an article from an April 25, 1891 China and Glassware Reporter: "The Rococo keeps jumping all over the factory. The plate is the lightest made in this country or imported, in earthenware. All the pieces are light, especially the flat pieces and every one is festooned, adding very much to their beauty. At these works they are making specialties in after dinner coffees and bone dishes". Rococo was produced as late as 1913.

Known items made in the Rococo shape: trade measurements
Bone dish
Bakers 7", 8"
Bowl 30s
Butter covered

Butter (pat) individual
Casseroles 7", 8"
Casserole notched
Cake plate
Chocolate pot
Cream
Covered dish 7", 8"
Dishes (platters) 8", 10", 12", 14", 16"
Jug 4s, 6s, 12s, 24s, 30s, 36s
Buffet jug
Nappies 7", 8"
Pickle
Plates flat 4", 5", 6", 7", 8"
Plates deep 6", 7"
Preserve 4", 5"
Sauce boat
Sugar covered
Tea cup/saucer

This list may was taken from an 1892 order for Rococo and may not be complete. Also sold with the Rococo shape were Cape Cod salads, Minton teacups, Ovide teas/ coffee cups and Saxon teas/coffee cups.

Rococo shape, Gold Band decoration. covered sugar $40-45

Rococo shapes from an early Homer Laughlin China Company catalog.

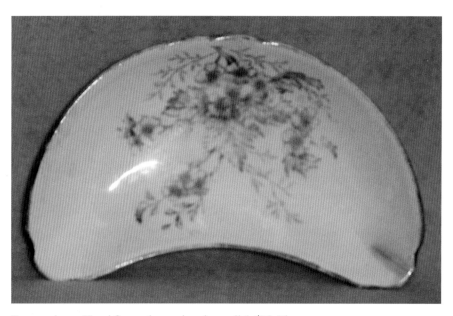

Rococo shape, Hazel Spray decoration. bone dish $18-25

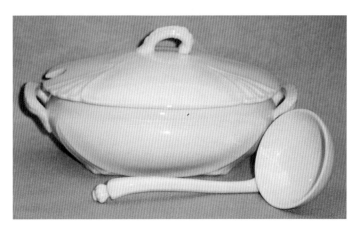

Rococo shape sauce tureen and ladle, Snow White undecorated. set complete $100-125

Rococo shape, Primrose Pinks decoration. plate $15-18, cup $10-15

Rose and Poppy

The Rose and Poppy decoration belonged to the Colgate Company and was sold from 1938 to about 1958.

Mixed shapes, Rose and Poppy decoration number K4124.

Round the Clock 1941

Round the Clock was a merchandising plan developed in 1941 as an exclusive promotion with the Allied stores. The plan utilized Georgian and Nautilus shapes in the following decorations: G-3351 Rosemont (called Cynthia when it sold to Wards), G-3330 Regent, G-3304 Duchess became Rose Lane when sold to Allied, N-1577 Ferndale, N-1590 Du Barry (also called Rosemary).

Royal Chrome 1937

The Homer Laughlin Company provided Fiesta® ware for the Royal Metal Company under the trade name of Royal Chrome. The Royal Metal Company added metal frames and sold these combined pieces in assortments, no open stock.

Royal Chrome Fiesta® pieces sold to Royal Metal Company in Fiesta glazes of Yellow, Light Green, Cobalt, and Red with the red pieces being more expensive.

Platter oval 13"
Casseroles round open 8 1/2", 9 1/2"
Casserole covered 8"
Pie plate round 10"
Condiment set- yellow mustard, blue pepper and green salt
Lug soup-sweet meat dish
Cake set, cake plate and cake lifter
Marmalade jar
Salad set-bowl and plates

Center Right:
1937 Royal Chrome brochure showing Fiesta® pieces in Royal Metal Company ware.

Right:
Royal Chrome brochure showing Fiesta® pieces in Royal Metal Company ware.

Royal Chrome red Fiesta® pie plate in metal frame with Royal Chrome colored ovenware sticker. No price established

Royal Majolica Scenic Dinnerware 1908

Royal Majolica is a decoration name and not a shape name. The decoration No. 390 was used on The Angelus, Colonial, and Hudson shapes produced by the Homer Laughlin China Company. The Palm Fetchteler decalcomania company produced the Royal Majolica in 1907 and 1908. It was an exclusive decoration of the Sears Roebuck Company. Each piece was elaborately decorated and was an exact reproduction of nature scenes such as farmhouses, bridges, dwellings with thatched roofs, rivers, oceans and country scenes in summer and winter. Each piece was stippled in genuine bright coin gold.

The Angelus shape covered casserole, Royal Majolica Scenic decoration number 390 for Sears & Roebuck. $75-95

Known pieces in The Angelus shape-Royal Majolica decoration

Butter covered
Casserole covered
Bowl fruit
Butter individual
Bowl oatmeal
Bowl vegetable
Pitcher
Plates 3 sizes
Relish
Platters 2 sizes
Bowl round vegetable
Sauceboat
Bowl soup
Bowl sugar
Cream
Tea cup/ saucer

The Angelus shape covered casserole, Royal Majolica Scenic decoration on the lid.

The Angelus shape, Royal Majolica Scenic
decoration. plates $15-18 each
covered butter $100-125

Royal OvenServe
1930s

The Homer Laughlin Company
provided decorated OvenServe
pieces for the Royal Metal Company
for use in their metal frame holders.

Royal OvenServe oval deep well platter,
Polychrome decoration. $35-38

Royal OvenServe oval deep well platter, Red
Clover decoration. $30-35

Royal OvenServe, Red Clover decoration. pie
plate $30-35
covered casserole $30-35

Saxon 1960s

Saxon is a short set of hollowware used with different flatware to make up sets of dinnerware. This was a common practice in the pottery industry.

Known pieces made in the Saxon shape:

Cup	Salt
Lug open butter	Pepper
Chop plate	Sauceboat
Cream	Bowl covered
Sugar	Coffee pot

Saxon shape from a Homer Laughlin catalog, Regal decoration.

Saxon shape cup, Regal decoration.

Saxon shape cream, cup, sauceboat, shakers, Solid White decoration.

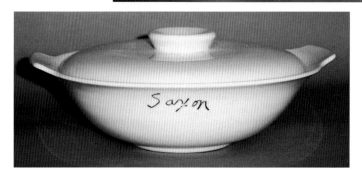

Saxon shape covered casserole, Solid White decoration.

Seneca 1901

The 1903 Sears catalog states: "Next to the celebrated English ware, this product of Homer Laughlin is considered the best in the market. Edges, handles and knobs are gold stippled, which gives the set a rich appearance". A 100-piece set was offered for $8.70.

Row 1: Item 1- individual butter, Item 2-bone dish, Item 3- sauce boat, Item 4-teapot, Item 5-sugar/cover, Item 6-cream, Item 7-jug

Row 2: Item 8-nappy, Item 9-bowl, Item 10-coffee cup/saucer, Item 11-tea cup/saucer, Item 12-pickle dish, Item 13-fruit bowl, Item 14-oatmeal bowl, Item 15-coupe soup

Row 3: Item 16-baker, Item 17-deep plate, Item 18-plate, Item 19-cake plate, Item 20-dish (platter)

Row 4: Item 21-casserole/cover, Item 22-dish covered, Item 23-butter/cover, Item 24-sauce tureen complete, Item 25-oyster tureen

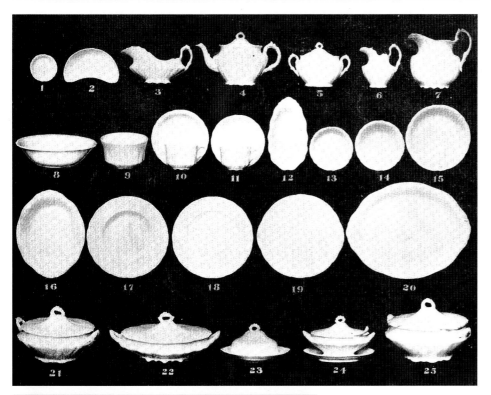

Seneca shapes from an old Homer Laughlin China Company catalog

Seneca shape pitcher, Holly and Berry decoration. $35-45

Seneca shape plate, Blue Corn-flower decoration. $15-18

Seneca shape sauceboat, Phlox decoration. $20-25

Seneca shape pitcher, Dutch Subjects decoration. $35-45

Seneca shape small pitcher, Snow White with initial decoration. $25-30

Serenade 1939

Serenade was introduced in January of 1939. The Homer Laughlin China Company advertised this shape, "The magic of delicate, soft pastel shades in yellow, pink, green and blue. The finish is soft and rich with a faintly dull glaze". Serenade is a very sought after pastel set. Much difficulty with the Serenade colors was encountered in the manufacture of this line of dinnerware. A letter dated November 24,1941 from Mr. J. D. Thompson of the Homer Laughlin China Company to Bechtel, Lutz and Jost said, "We have just decided that after January 1,1942 we are going to discontinue the manufacture of Serenade dinnerware. You know it has never been a great success-it is difficult to make, very hard to keep uniform, and due to conditions now it is just necessary that we drop everything that is not a quantity production". A 7 1/2" casserole body was sold to the Royal Metal Manufacturing Company in 1939. A Homer Laughlin Company order shows the casserole body offered in white, yellow, pink and blue. This piece even though it is marked Serenade is not a part of the Serenade set. It was made to fit a Royal metal frame and the lid was more than likely also provided by the Royal Metal Company. A few Laughlin lids have surfaced that fit this bowl.

Known pieces made in the Serenade shape: actual measurements

Plate chop 13"	Platter oval 12"
Plate 10"	Pickle dish/gravy boat liner
Plate 9"	Nappy 8 1/2"
Plate 7"	Creamer
Plate 6"	Sugar covered
Plate deep 8"	Gravy/sauce boat
Bowl lug soup	Salt shaker
Bowl cereal/fruit 5"	Pepper shaker
Tea cup	Teapot covered
Tea saucer	Casserole covered

Senerade shape. sauceboat $40-45
teapot $90-95
sugar $20-25
cream $15-20

Serenade shape. lug soup $25-30
small plate $12-15
9" plate $16-18
fruit $8-10
shakers $25-30 pair
cup and saucer $18-20

Serenade shape from a Homer Laughlin catalog, Aster decoration number RUM-703.

Below:
Serenade shape from a Homer Laughlin catalog, Cosmos decoration number RUM-700.

Serenade 1962

Serenade is also the name of a line introduced in the 1960s and the only similarity to the 1937 Serenade is in the name. The back stamp on this Serenade ware reads "hand decorated, oven proof, detergent proof. Homer Laughlin Made in U.S.A.". The words "detergent proof" are an excellent clue that this is a later ware.

Known pieces made in the 1960s Serenade dinnerware line: actual measurements
Tea cup- color outside
Tea saucer -decorated
Plate dinner 10"- decorated
Plate pie or salad plate 7"- decorated
Plate bread & butter 6"-decorated
Soup cereal 5 3/4"- color inside
Fruit/dessert - color inside
Bowl round vegetable- color inside
Platter 13 1/2"- decorated
Sugar covered -color outside
Cream- color outside
Sauceboat-color inside

Serenade shape from a Homer Laughlin catalog, Orchard decoration number RUM-701.

Left:
Senerade shape from a Homer Laughlin catalog, Tulip decoration number RUM702.

Serenade shape plate, Country Fair decoration.
$7-10

Shakespeare 1885

The Shakespeare shape was in all probability named for Homer Laughlin's younger brother Shakespeare who died in 1881. Mr. A. Brocoff, decorator employed by the Homer Laughlin China Company decorated most of the Shakespeare pieces. An ad that appeared for the Shakespeare shape in the August 2, 1885 issue of Crockery and Glass Journal states: "Stocked in plain white and decorated ware. Homer Laughlin being the only white ware manufacturer in East Liverpool owning a railroad siding at my works and have special facilities for safely packing full car loads in bulk which saves the usual cost of package to my wholesale customers. Catalogs, discounts, etc. furnished applicants."

Known pieces made in the Shakespeare shape: trade measurements

A.D. cup	Pickle/relish
A.D. saucer	Plates three sizes
Casserole covered	Sauceboat
Cup coffee	Sauce tureen and liner
Cup saucer	Bowl serving
Cream	Sugar covered
Bowl fruit	Tea cup/saucer
Jugs open, two sizes	Teapot

Shakespeare shape, Gold Band decoration. cream $15-20
covered casserole $65-75
cup $8-10
saucer 6-8
plate $15-18

Shakespeare shape, from an old Homer Laughlin catalog, Cardinal decoration.

Shakespeare shape covered sauce tureen, Morning Glory decoration. $35-45

Shakespeare shape teapot, Passion Flower decoration. $100-125

Shakespeare Country 1967

See Brittany.

Sheffield 1970s

Sheffield is a trade name for dinnerware lines produced in the 1970s for the J and H International Company, who specialized in products for super market premium and continuity lines. Dinnerware items were made by many companies both in and out of this country and marketed under the Sheffield name. The Jepcor Company was an offshoot of the J and H International Company. Jepcor was later taken over by the Noritake Company, a new division of J & H was then developed and became Newcor.

Sheffield trademark

Skytone 1950

Skytone is a modern design used on the Jubilee shape and advertised as "America's Newest Dinnerware Creation in a subtle sky blue body with handles in snow white". A few stylized decorations were applied to this shape designed by Don Schreckengost.

Known items made in Skytone: trade measurements

Tea cup and saucer	Chop plate 11"
Plate 8"	Sugar covered
Plate 7"	Cream
Plate 5"	Casserole covered
Plate 4"	Sauceboats, fast stands
Coupe 7"	Coffee pots, covered
Lug soup	Tea pots, covered
Fruit	A.D. Coffee cups/saucers
Nappy 7"	Salt Shakers
Dish (platter) 12"	Pepper Shakers
Dish (platter) 10"	Double Egg Cups
Dish (platter) 8"	

Skytone coffeepot $35-45
covered sugar $15-20

Staples 1900s

Potteries had a group of ware that were called staple items. They were plain white or decorated individually and could be used in other lines. The White Granite staple items shown are from a 1916 Homer Laughlin China Company catalog. There were items other than what is shown here such as cake dishes, soda mugs, single and double eggcups, baby cups and baby plates. The collector can expect to find many different sizes of nappies, jugs, bakers, bowls and dishes (platters) in all of these old shapes including the dinnerware shapes.

Row 1: Item 1- sauce boat, Item 2- sick feeder, Item 3- pap boat, Item 4- sugar/cover, Item 5- spooner, Item 6- single egg cup, Item 7- double egg cup, Item 8- Sapho molasses can, Item 9- Cable molasses can

Row 2: Item 10-fruit bowl, Item 11-coffee mug Baltimore, Item 12-scallop nappy, Item 13-oyster bowl, Item 14-bird bath, Item 15-mustard/cover, Item 16-covered butter

Row 3: Item 17-Home tea, Item 18-Home coffee, Item 19-Baltimore tea, Item 20-St. Denis tea small, Item 21-St. Denis tea, Item 22-St. Denis coffee, Item 23-Newell tea, Item 24-Waldorf tea, Item 25-Virginia jug, Item 26-St. Denis bowl, Item 27-cake cover, Item 28-plate, Item 29-dish (platter), Item 30-baker

Row 4: Item 31-punch bowl, Item 32-mixing bowl, Item 33-fluted comport, Item 34-fluted nappy, Item 35-Cable jug

THE HOMER LAUGHLIN CHINA COMPANY, NEWELL, W. VA.

WHITE GRANITE STAPLES.

Staples shapes from old Homer Laughlin Company catalog

Star-Brite 1950s

The Star-Brite line is a continuation of the original Dura-Print decoration. Star-Brite was advertised as "smart contemporary styling." Star-Brite like Dura-Print is a combination of the Rhythm shape flatware and Charm House hollowware.

Known Star-Brite items: actual measurements
Cup/saucer
Bowl dessert 5 1/2"
Bowl soup 8"
Plate salad 7 1/2"
Plate bread and butter 6 1/4"
Creamer
Sugar and cover
Platter 11 1/2"
Nappy vegetable 7"
Gravy boat

UNIT A
1 each 9" coupe shape plate
1 each cup – 1 each saucer
1 each 5½" dessert dish

UNIT B
1 each 8" soup plate
1 each 7½" salad plate
1 each 6¼" bread and butter dish

STAR-BRITE OVEN-PROOF WARES
in smart contemporary styling
★ original dura-print pattern never washes off, even in dishwasher
★ in modern coupe shape

you can build up to service for 8 or 12 with additional units A, B and C

see other side for units B and C

STAR-BRITE OVEN-PROOF WARES
in smart contemporary styling

UNIT C
1 each creamer
1 each sugar bowl
1 each cover for sugar bowl
1 each large 11½" platter
1 each 7" vegetable nappy
1 each gravy boat

Star-Brite from a Homer Laughlin Company catalog

Studio 1957

The Studio line was a short set of hollow ware produced to go with other set compositions, mainly the Dura-Print line. Some pieces of Studio hollowware had pink, yellow or turquoise tints inside. Studio can also be found without the tinted colors inside.

Known Studio pieces are a cup, cream, sugar and cover

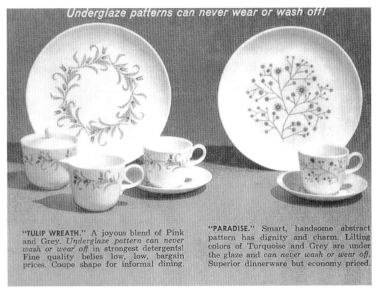

Studio shape from a Homer Laughlin Company catalog. Left to right, Tulip Wreath decoration, Paradise decoration

Studio shape from a 1957 Homer Laughlin China Company catalog, Pink Magnolia decoration.

Sunrise 1929

The Sunrise trademark was used exclusively in 1929 and 1930 by Sears Roebuck to advertise dinnerware. The Laughlin shapes sold under the Sunrise trademark were Republic, Yellowstone, Empress, Kwaker and Newell. The following advertisement appeared in a 1930 catalog for some of the Homer Laughlin shapes sold under the Sunrise mark.

"Sunrise" is made in the world's largest and most scientifically equipped pottery from the best clays and glazes obtainable, producing in the finished products a degree of excellence usually not approached in dinnerware sold elsewhere at such low prices. "Sunrise" is strictly hand-picked, first selection American china (semi-porcelain). The "Sunrise" brand is placed only on first quality dinnerware.

Sunrise Brand Dinnerware backstamp

Suntone 1950

Suntone is the same shape as the Jubilee shape. It has a rich red tinted body, which comes from natural clay introduced into the body. Suntone has white handles and knobs. Company records do not indicate decorations added to the Suntone line. One of the favorites of the Suntone line is the small mini-cup and saucer set that was a give-a-way at trade shows.

Known items made in Suntone: actual sizes

Tea cup/saucer	
Plate 10"	Sugar covered
Plate 9"	Cream
Plate 7 1/4"	Casserole covered
Plate 6"	Sauceboat fast stand
Bowl soup coupe 8"	Coffee pot covered
Bowl soup lug	Teapot covered
Bowl fruit 5 1/2"	Coffee cup/saucer A.D.
Nappy 7 1/2"	Salt
Dish (platter)15 1/2"	Pepper
Dish (platter)13 1/2"	Egg cup
Dish (platter)11 1/2"	Mini-cup/saucer
Plate chop 14 1/2"	

Suntone teapot $45-55
coffeepot $45-55
sugar $15-18

Swing 1938

Swing was advertised as "Music in tableware, a new high-spirited shape to suit the tempo of the times. Swing is distinguished by its simple, modern, smooth-gliding lines and its dynamic, youthful appeal. It is made in the famous Eggshell, remarkable for its light weight, its delicacy, and its craze-proof glaze. Simplicity and style are the keynotes of Swing patterns." Mist Blue, Coral (also called Salmon) and Light Green glazes were applied to the graceful circular handles. Frederick Rhead designed the Swing shape. The Swing shape patent number 402,262 was filed on January 24, 1938.

Swing shape, America The Beautiful
series decoration. cup $8-10
small plate $6-8
soup $10-14
plate $12-15

Known pieces made in the Swing shape: trade measurements
Cup/ saucer
Plate dinner 7", 8", 9", 10"
Plate bread & butter 4"
Bowl fruit 4"
Bowl coupe soup 8"
Platter 8 3/4"x 11 1/4"
Sauce boat
Sugar covered
Cream
Casserole covered
Teapot
Tray oblong
Muffin cover
Salt and pepper shakers
Egg cup Cable shape
Vegetable oval
Cream soup and liner
A.D. sugar and cream
A.D. cup and saucer
A.D. coffee pot

Swing shape, close up of plate, America
The Beautiful series decoration

Swing shape plates. Left to right, Avon decoration, Lily of the Valley decoration. $10-14 each

Swing shape plate, Cardinal decoration. $10-14

Swing shape plate, Chinese Buddha decoration number S152P. $15-18

Swing shape, Chinese Green Goddess decoration S157G. serving bowl $20-25
platters $25-30
plates $15-18
cup and saucer $15-20

Swing shape, Chinese Porcelain decoration
platter $25-30
fruit $6-10
sugar $20-24
cream $18-20

Swing shape, Chinese Princess decoration. bowl $20-25
platter $25-30
plate $15-18
fruit $6-10
cream $18-20
cup and saucer $18-20

Below:
Swing shape, Chinese Willow decoration. plate $15-18
bowl $20-25
plate $15-18
cup and saucer $18-20

Swing shape serving bowl, Chinese Three decoration. $20-25

Swing shape plates. Left to right Colonial decoration, Wayside decoration. $10-14 each

Swing shape plate, Colonial Kitchen decoration S129. $14-18

Swing shape teapot, Colonial Kitchen decoration. $70-80

Swing shape plate, Della Robbia decoration. $10-12

Swing shape, Doll's House decoration. fruit $5-8
plate $10-12
platter $22-25
baker $16-20
small plate $7-9
saucer and cup $15-18

Swing shape plate, Gardenia decoration. $10-12

Swing shape plate, Greenbriar/Heather
Lane decoration. $10-12

Swing shape cup, saucer, International/.Swedish Modern decoration.
$10-14

Swing shape bowl, LaPetite decorationnumber S113. $10-14

Swing shape cup, saucer, Mexicana
Variation decoration. $18-22

Swing shape plate, Sovereign decoration. $10-12

Swing shape, Moss Rose decoration number S163.
After Dinner sugar $10-12
After Dinner cream $10-12
After Dinner teapot $15-35

Swing shape plate with Omar decoration, from the Homer
Laughlin morgue. No price established

Swing shape plate from the Homer Laughlin morgue, S112 decoration number. No price established

Tablefair

see Harlequin / Tablefair

Tango 1936

The Tango shape was designed by Frederick Rhead and released in 1936. Tango was made in solid colors only of Burgundy, Yellow, Green, Blue and Orange/Red. It was sold to J.J. Newberry and McLellan five and dime stores. Tango was also used as premium items. The Tango shape and the Riviera shape share the same shape of salt and pepper shakers.

Known Tango pieces: actual measurements
Bowl fruit 5 1/2"
Baker 9"
Nappy 8 3/4"
Casserole

Cream
Sugar covered
Plates 6", 7", 8", 9", 10"
Plate deep 6"
Platter 11 3/4"
Tea cup/saucer
Salt and pepper shakers
Egg cup

Tango shape cream $25-30
plate $25-30
sugar $25-30
shakers $10-14
cup and saucer $30-35

Tea Rose 1937

Tea Rose was produced as a premium offer for the Quaker Oats Company.
Known Tea Rose pieces: actual measurements
Tea cup
Saucer
Bowl fruit 5 1/2"
Bowl oatmeal
Nappy
Plate 9 1/4", 8 1/4", 7 1/4", 4 1/4"
Platter 11 2/3"

Tea Rose shape cup, saucer, decoration W5923. $10-12

Tea Rose shape plates. Left to right, Rose and Starflower decoration, Medallion decoration. $6-8 each

Tempo 1960s

The Tempo shape was modeled in 1964. Listed are a sugar body- cover and knob, a cream, cup and handle, coffee server body and knob, sauceboat and utility jug. No other information could be found concerning this shape.

The Angelus

See Angelus

Theme 1939

The Theme shape was designed to exhibit at the 1939 New York World's Fair. The shape was described as having a rich embossed border of fruit design in light- weight, and was decorated with old- fashioned floral centers of modern colorings. The Theme shape dinnerware had the charm of old English gardens, which appealed to the most discriminating buyers.

Known pieces made in the Theme shape: trade measurements

A.D. cup	Plates 8", 7", 6", 5", 4"
A.D. saucer	Plate deep 6"
Baker	Plate square 6"
Casserole covered	Salt and Pepper set
Dish (platters) 12", 10", 8"	Sauceboat regular
Plate chop 11"	Sauceboat fast stand
Pickle dish 6"	Sugar covered
Cream	Tea cup/saucer
Cream soup cup/saucer	Teapot covered
Onion soup (lugged oatmeal)	

Theme shapes from Homer Laughlin China Company.

Theme shape, Heather Lane/Argyle/Florentine decoration number TH6. saucer $5-7
sauceboat $12-15

Theme shape plate, Cameo decoration. $8-10

Theme shape, Mexicali Variation decoration. plate $10-12
saucer $5-8

Theme shape plate, Pink Magnolia decoration. $10-12

Theme shape plate from the Homer Laughlin morgue, decoration number TH 34. No price established

Theme shape plate, Regency decoration number VM104 for Vogue Mercantile. $10-12

Theme shape plate, Surrey decoration number TH17. $10-12

Theme shape plate, bowl, cup and saucer from Homer Laughlin catalog, Vintage decoration. No price established

Theme shape plate from the Homer Laughlin morgue, decoration number TH 24. No price established

Toiletries 1884 -late 1920s

Toiletry sets were popular and necessary items before the widespread use of indoor plumbing. They were available in a variety of shapes and decorations and came in 6-10-12 piece sets. Toiletry sets were probably made at the Laughlin's Ohio Valley Pottery from its beginning (1874) but we were only able to document toiletry items from 1884 in the company records. For more information on toiletry shapes and names see *Homer Laughlin China A Giant Among Dishes 1873-1939* by Jo Cunningham.

Trellis shape plates. Left to right, green glaze, yellow glaze, and white with green line decorations. $6-8 each

Trellis 1929

Trellis is one of several shapes designed for the Quaker Oats Company, but was later sold to other companies. To keep up with the demand of sales to Quaker Oats, the Trellis shape was also produced by other potteries. Each pottery was assigned a letter of the alphabet, usually the first letter of their pottery name to be added under the word "Trellis" as a backstamp. Trellis was produced in ivory, yellow and green solid color glazes as well as being decorated with a variety of decorations.

Known pieces made in the Trellis shape: trade measurements

Baker 7"	Bowl fruit 4"
Bowl deep	Nappy 7"
Plate cake 11"	Jugs open, five sizes
Casserole covered	Plates 4", 6", 7", 9"
Soup coupe 6"	Sauceboat
Cream	Tea cup/saucer
Dish (platters) 8", 9", 10"	Teapot

Trellis shape, decoration number T24. plate $8-10 cup and saucer $10-12

Trellis shape teapot, yellow with orange trim decoration. $85-100

Trellis shape plate from the morgue, decoration number T26. No price established

Trellis shape plates, decoration numbers T4 and T93. From the morgue. No price established

Trellis shape plates from the morgue. Left to right, decoration numbers T-48 and T-50. No price established

Trellis shape plates from the morgue. Left to right, decoration numbers T-91 and T-95. No price established

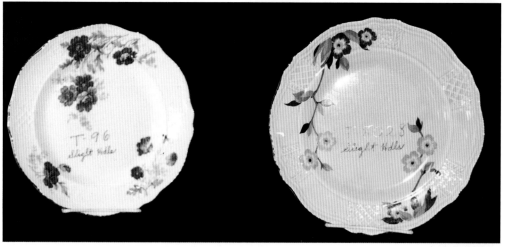

Trellis shape, decoration numbers T96 and T8028. From the morgue. No price established

Trellis shape, decoration number QO10 for
Quaker Oats. open sugar $8-10
plate $8-10
cream $8-10

Triumph 1959

The Triumph shape was one of the last shapes designed by Don Schreckengost for The Homer Laughlin China Company. The sleek, smooth lines combined Old World Charm and New World Simplicity, according to the Triumph brochures. Triumph featured a swan-like background with simple lines.

Known Triumph pieces: actual measurements
Tea cup
Tea saucer
Plate dinner 10"
Plate salad 8"
Plate bread and butter 6"
Bowl coupe soup 8"
Bowl fruit/dessert 5 1/4"
Platters 13 1/8", 11 1/4"
Bowls vegetable 8 1/4", 7 3/4"
Sugar covered
Creamer
Sauceboat
Pickle/relish dish
Casserole covered
Coffee pot and cover
A.D. Coffee cup and saucer
Salt and pepper set

Trellis shape pieces made for Quaker Oats

Triumph shapes from Homer Laughlin catalog

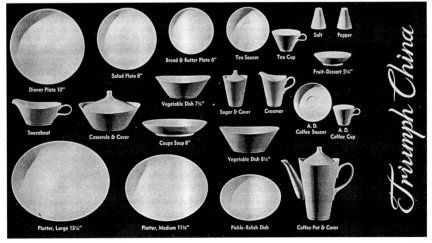

Triumph shape from Homer Laughlin catalog: top left: Linda decoration number TR-7, top right: Woodland decoration number TR3: lower left: October decoration number TR6: lower right Spring Rose decoration number TR1.

Triumph shape, rim detail and October decoration.

Triumph shape from Homer Laughlin catalog. Left: June Rose decoration number TR9. Right: Autumn Time decoration number TR10

Triumph shape plate from the Homer Laughlin morgue, decoration number TR12. No price established

TRIUMPH CHINA. Brilliantly pure white . . . Fully vitrified and translucent . . . . For . . . Every-Day and Every-Meal use or for Formal Occasions . . . Strongest casual china made . . . . Every piece . . . . GUARANTEED FOR A YEAR AGAINST BREAKAGE BY . . . HOMER LAUGHLIN.

Triumph
HOMER LAUGHLIN

"JUNE ROSE." True *Triumph* China. Wreaths of delicate pink rosebuds are accented by stylized Grey stems and leaves. *Platinum* trim on every piece adds richness.

"AUTUMN TIME." True *Triumph* China. Adds cheer to every meal. Gay, happy colors of bright Orange, Brown, Blue and Yellow, captures the glory of Fall. Trimmed with *22K Gold*.

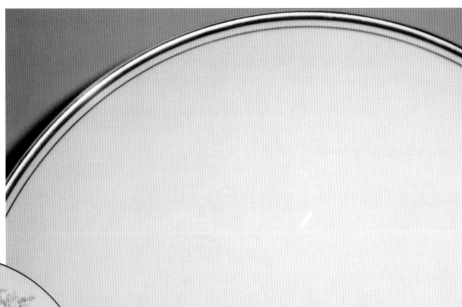

Triumph shape plate from the Homer Laughlin morgue, decoration number TR30. No price established

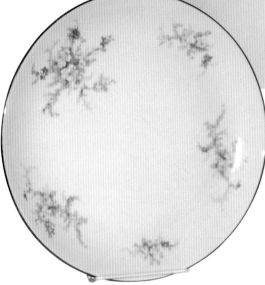

Triumph shape plate from the Homer Laughlin morgue, decoration number TR35. No price established

In the 1960s a line advertised as Triumph Snow White China was used as a premium for the Von's Grocery Store. The Von's Triumph China appears to be a mix of the American China and Triumph shapes. The American China pieces are backstamped Triumph Snow White and the same backstamp was used on these pieces as the original 1959 Triumph line even though the shapes are different. (see American China)

Known pieces offered in Von's Triumph line: actual measurements

Plate dinner 10"	Bowl vegetable
Plate bread and butter	Bowl soup/cereal
Plate salad	Bowl dessert/fruit
Platter oval 13"	Creamer
Gravy/sauce boat	Sugar covered
Cup and saucer	Pickle/relish

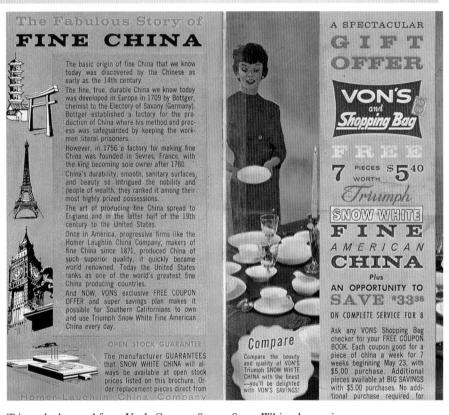

Triumph shape ad from Von's Grocery Store, Snow White decoration.

Triumph shape, Snow White decoration. sugar $8-12
American China shape, Snow White decoration. cream $6-8

Tudor Rose 1930s

The Tudor Rose is not the name of a Homer Laughlin shape but was a line made for the Quaker Oats Company in the late 1930s and early 1940s and is most often found on the Wells shape. It was first thought to be the name of the decoration, we now know that there is more than one decoration used with the Tudor Rose mark.

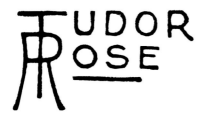

Tudor Rose backstamp

Tudor Rose cream $10-12
sugar $12-15

Victor shape covered butter, solid white decoration. $45-55

Victor 1883

The Victor shape was one that seemed to turn the corner in making the Homer Laughlin China Company a success. Not only was it produced in dinnerware sets but also in toiletry sets. Some sources refer to the finials as an attempt to utilize the HL trademark. The Victor was a popular shape and produced for many years. The Victor shape seems to be a mixture of the Cable shape and Victor.

Victor shape celery holder, pink flowers with gold trim decoration. $85-95

Victor shape covered casserole, solid white decoration. $65-75

Victoria 1960s

Vincent Broomhall designed the Victoria shape in the 1960s. Victoria is a white, swirl shape marketed under the Sheffield name and was also offered in various premium stamp catalogs. The Arcadia decoration on Victoria was offered in a 1966 S&H stamp book. The 45- piece set was offered for 7 1/2 books, the 20-piece set was 2 3/4 books.

Known Victoria pieces:

Cup
Saucer
Plate dinner
Plate bread and butter
Bowl fruit
Bowl soup

Bowl vegetable
Platter meat
Sugar covered
Cream

Victoria shape plate, cup and saucer from an old ad, Arcadia decoration.

Victoria shapes Silver Swirl decoration number V-110 and Blossom Time decoration number V123. $6-8

Victoria shape plate from the Homer Laughlin morgue, decoration number V117 for McDonald Stamps. No price established

Victoria shape plate from the Homer Laughlin morgue, decoration number GM114 for Murphy Company. No price established

Virginia Rose 1933

The Virginia Rose shape has embossed roses spaced around the rim, and was produced on a white or yellow glaze body. Hundreds of different decorations were used on the Virginia Rose shape from its introduction in 1933 until well into the 1960s. Virginia Rose was designed by Frederick Rhead and was named after a granddaughter of Mr. W. E. Wells. The shape was well received by the consumer and an entire plant (#8) was built to accommodate its production. Virginia Rose continues to be a popular shape with collectors.

Known pieces made in the Virginia Rose shape: trade measurements

Bakers 6", 7", 8"
Bowl 36s
Butter covered
Plate cake
Casserole covered
Cream soup cup/saucer
Bowl coupe 7"
Dish (platters) 7", 8", 10", 12"
Double egg cup (Cable shape)
Bowls 4", 5"
Nappies 6", 7"
Nappy 8" (for Colgate and J.J. Newberry)
Bowl oatmeal 36s
Onion soup (Nautilus Regular lug soup)
Jugs open 24s, 42s (for J.J. Newberry)
Pickle 6"
Plates 4", 5", 6", 7", 8"
Plate 6" square, Cunningham & Pickett
Plate deep 6"
Sauceboat regular
Sauceboat fast stand
Nappy salad
Shakers (Swing shape)
Sugar covered
Tea cup/saucer

Virginia Rose shape platter, Bluebonnets decoration number VR420. $25-28

Virginia Rose shape plate, Colonial Kitchen decoration. $10-15

Virginia Rose shape plates. Left to right, Bouquet decoration number VR137, Spring Wreath decoration number CAC186. $10-12 each

Virginia Rose shape plate, Dresden decoration. $8-10

Virginia Rose shape cream, Gold Rose decoration number VR115. $8-12

Virginia Rose shape plate, Petit Point decoration. $10-12

Virginia Rose shape plate, Louise decoration number VR390. $10-12

Virginia Rose shape plates. Left to right, Pink Wild Flower decoration, decoration number VR387. $10-12 each

Virginia Rose shape plates. Left to right, Nosegay decoration number VR423, Wild Rose decoration number VR269. $10-12 each

Virginia Rose shape covered casserole, undecorated. $20-25

Virginia Rose shape plate, Sunporch decoration. $20-25

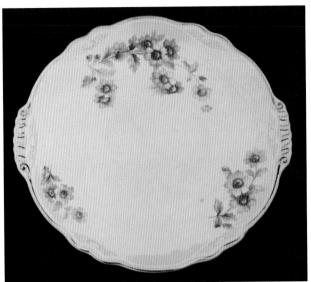

Virginia Rose shape cake plate, decoration number JJ59. $25-35

Virginia Rose shape plates from the morgue. Left to right, decoration numbers VR101, VR104, VR105, VR106. No price established

Virginia Rose shape, Tulips in a Basket decoration number VR412. $10-12

Virginia Rose shape plates from the morgue. Left to right, decoration numbers VR114, VR115. No price established

Virginia Rose shape plates from the morgue. Left to right, back row decoration numbers VR118, VR119, VR120. Left to right, front row decoration numbers: VR121, VR122, VR132. No price established

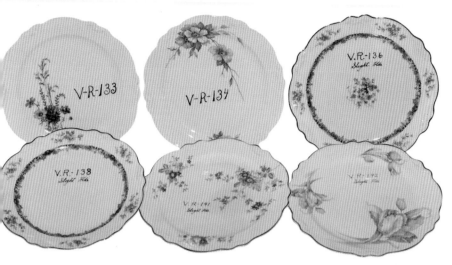

Virginia Rose shape plates from the morgue. Left to right, back row decoration numbers VR133, VR134, VR136. Left to right, front row decoration numbers VR 138, VR141, VR142. No price established

Virginia Rose shape plate, decoration number VR158. $10-12

Virginia Rose shape plate, decoration number VR135. $10-12

Virginia Rose shape, decoration number VR172.
small plate $8-10
large plate $10-12
cup and saucer $10-12
covered sugar $18-20

Virginia Rose shape plates from the morgue. Left to right, back row decoration numbers VR143, VR151, VR152: Left to right, front row decoration numbers VR153, VR155, VR162. No price established

Virginia Rose shape plates. Left to right, decoration number VR232, decoration number VR440. $10-12 each

Virginia Rose shape covered jug, decoration number VR394. $55-65

Left:
Virginia Rose shape plate, decoration number VR399. $10-12

Below:
Virginia Rose shape plates. Left to right, decoration number VR437, decoration number VR245. $10-12

Virginia Rose shape baker, decoration number VR316. $15-18

Left:
Virginia Rose shape plate, decoration number VR341. $10-12

Below:
Virginia Rose shape sauceboat, decoration number VR365. $15-18

Below: Virginia Rose shape plates. Left to right, decoration number VR456, decoration number VR452. $10-12 each

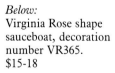

Vogue 1963

The Vogue is a modern, plain shape made for the F. W. Woolworth's Company and was new for 1963. A Vogue shape coffee pot was one of the items included in the Homer Laughlin China exhibit at the West Virginia State Museum Department of Culture and History, Charleston, West Virginia from March 1985 through March of 1987. This Vogue shape has no connection with the American Vogue or Vogue Mercantile.

Known Vogue pieces:

Cup	Cream
Coffee server	Sugar

Vogue shape small plates, marked F. W. Woolworth, decoration blue and gray on white body. $6-8

Vogue shape sugar, cream, and cup, decoration in blue and white. No price established

Vogue shape divided baker, decoration in blue and white. No price established

Right:
Vogue shape 1966 trade journal ad, Autumn Fantasy decoration.

THE HOMER LAUGHLIN CHINA COMPANY. An "Autumn Fantasy" of color is evident in this leaf spray on Vogue-shaped dinnerware, with harmonizing solid color pieces; ovenproof, dishwasher safe. A 45-piece service is $24.95, retail.

Vogue Mercantile Company, Vogue and American Vogue

The Vogue Mercantile Company was a large distributor of glass and pottery. Located in New York City, they purchased dinnerware from companies like Homer Laughlin, Universal Pottery and others and then resold the dinnerware. In 1949, the Vogue Mercantile Company was renamed Vogue Ceramic Industries. Phillip Distillator of the Jackson China Company was owner of the Vogue Mercantile and Vogue Ceramic Industries. Many different Homer Laughlin shapes were sold under the Vogue backstamp.

American Vogue/ American Vogue Mercantile Company backstamp, Regency decoration

Wells 1930

The Wells shape had decals applied before the solid matte glazes of Leaf Green, French Rose, Sienna Brown and a limited production of Melon Yellow. The shape was named for the Homer Laughlin's Chairman of the Board, Mr. W. E. Wells, who had resigned his position the same year. The Wells shape was exhibited for the first time on January 13,1930 at the 50th Annual Pottery Show in the Fort Pitt and Williams Hotel in Pittsburgh, Pennsylvania.

Known pieces made in the Wells shape: actual measurements

A.D. cup
A.D. saucer
Baker 9"
Batter set, 3 pieces (covered jug 9", open syrup 4", tray)
Bowl cream soup
Bowl fruit 5"
Bowl oatmeal 36s
Butter individual
Casserole covered
Coffee cup
Coffeepot individual 5"
Jug covered 9"
Cream
Soup cream

Bouillon cup, handled
Egg cup double
Pickle dish, handled
Plate chop, handled
Muffin cover
Plates 6", 7" 9", 10"
Plate deep
Plate square 6"
Platters oval 11 1/2", 13 1/2", 15 1/2"
Sauceboat and liner
Sauceboat fast stand
Sugar individual (open)
Sugar covered
Syrup jug 4"
Teapot

Wells shape, Sienna Brown, Wells colored glaze. fruit $12-15
plate $14-18
cup and saucer $18-24

Wells shape, Tulip decoration number W5623.

Wells shape, Wells colored glazes. Left to right, small plates, Melon Yellow $6-8 each
Sienna Brown lug soup and liner $22-25
Leaf Green cream $20-24
Sienna Brown pitcher $100-120
individual cream $20-24
Melon Yellow cup and saucer $18-24
Sienna Brown small plates $6-8
nappy and platter $30-35 each
Leaf Green eggcup $20-24
individual teapot $90-100

Wells shape covered casserole, Rose color. $65-75

Wells shape teapot, Blue Willow decoration. $85-100

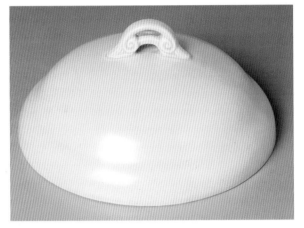

Wells shape muffin cover, Melon Yellow. $70-75

Right:
Wells shape plate,
Flight of the Swallows
decoration number
W4523. $14-18

Wells shape plate, Black Crocus decoration. $10-12

Wells shape casserole lid, Flowers of the Dell decoration. $10-12

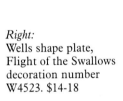

Right:
Wells shape, Gold Stripe decoration for
Sears Roebuck. small plate $4-6
large plate $6-8
sugar $8-10
cream $8-10

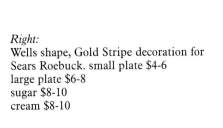

Wells shape platter, Modern Laurel decoration for Montgomery Ward. $14-16

Wells shape serving plate, Petit Point decoration, platinum trim. $18-20

Wells shape, Victoria decoration. small plate $8-10 sauceboat $15-18

Wells shape plates from the Homer Laughlin morgue. Left to right, decoration number FW12, decoration number FW13. No price established

Wells shape plates from the Homer Laughlin morgue. Left to right, decoration number W106, decoration number HUC2. No price established

Wells shape plates from the Homer Laughlin morgue. Left to right, decoration numbers W104, W106, W113. No price established

Wells shape, decoration W1133 Variation.
sauceboat $15-18
luncheon plate $8-10
sauceboat liner $10-12

Wells shape plates. Left to right, back row decoration numbers W2133, W5533, W7923. Left to right, front row decoration numbers W8033, W8523, W9423. From the morgue. No price established

Wells shape, Palm Tree decoration number W7923. cream $10-12
individual teapot $35-45
open sugar $15-18

Wells shape plates. Left to right decoration
number 2333, decoration number 2533. No
price established

Wells shape plates. Left to right decoration
numbers W4970, W5033, W5270. No price
established

Wells shape plates from the Homer Laughlin morgue. Left to right
decoration numbers W5433, W5670, W8923. No price established

Left:
Wells shape A.D. cup and saucer,
decoration number W5923. $25-35

Wells shape casserole, decoration number 9477. $55-65

Wells shape beverage mugs and tray. No price available

Wild Rose

see Quaker Oats

Wild Rose decoration covered sugar, cream made for Quaker Oats. Five different pieces were made for Quaker Oats to place in their oatmeal boxes: A 6 3/4" dessert, 6 1/4" cereal, 5 3/4" fruit bowl and a tea cup and saucer. Other serving pieces were available for sale.

Willow 1942

The Willow shape hollowware was designed to mix with other shapes of flat ware. The Willow shape was used in combination with the Americana, Blue and Pink Fantasy and Blue and Pink Willow. Flat ware used in the mixed set compositions were the Wells, Brittany and Empress shapes.

Mixed shapes, Blue Willow decoration from the Homer Laughlin China Company files.

Known pieces in the Willow shape:

Cup	Sugar
Saucer	Cream
Sauceboat	Milk pitcher

Willow decoration: Blue and Pink Willow 1935-1960s

The Willow decoration was first made by the Homer Laughlin China Company in 1935 and given the designation number W-435. Willow was another mixed shape set so common with the pottery industry. It was made in both pink and blue with the blue being more available. The list is from company orders and set compositions and collectors may find the Willow decoration on other Homer Laughlin shapes.

Willow Shapes: trade measurements
Jumbo cup
Teacup
Cream
Sugar covered (finial on cover is Willow shape)
Sauceboat
Jug 36s

Empress Shapes
Saucer tea
Bowl 36s
Nappy 7"
Bowl oatmeal (not the same as the 36s)
Casserole covered
Bowl fruit 4"
Soup coupe
Baker 7"

Empress shape covered casserole, Blue Willow decoration. $65-75

Empress shape large platter, Blue Willow Variant decoration. $45-50

Brittany Shapes
Plate deep (soup) 6"
Plates 4", 5", 7", 8"
Pickle dish
Dish (platters) 8", 10", 12"

Wells Shapes
Teapot (knob cover is Willow shape)
Plates 9", 10"

Wells shape teapot, Blue Willow decoration. $85-100

Yellowstone 1927

The Yellowstone shape broke the tradition of the round shapes of dinnerware with its octagon shape and creamy ivory or white body. Yellowstone was so popular that additional plants had to be built to accommodate the demand. The unusual octagon shape was a fresh idea to the dinnerware market and possessed warmth that appealed to consumers. Many different decorations were applied during Yellowstone's long production run.

Known items made in the Yellowstone shape: trade measurements
Item 1-tea cup/saucer, Item 2-coffee cup/saucer, Item 3- after dinner coffee cup/saucer, Item 4- jug 24s, Item 5- cream, Item 6- sugar/cover, Item 7- bowl 36s, Item 8- baker 7", Item 9- grapefruit, Item 10- coupe 7", Item 11- covered butter, Item 12- pickle, Item 13- relish, Item 14- casserole, Item 15- plate 7", Item 16- fruit 4", Item 17- dish/platter 8", Item 18- oatmeal, Item 19- nappy 7"

YELLOWSTONE DINNER SERVICE

1 Tea	4 Jug, 24s	8 Baker, 7 inch	12 Pickle	16 Fruit, 4 inch
2 Coffee	5 Cream	9 Grape Fruit	13 Relish	17 Dish, 8 inch
3 A. D. Coffee	6 Sugar	10 Coupe, 7 inch	14 Casserole	18 Oatmeal
	7 Bowl, 36s	11 Covered Butter	15 Plate, 7 inch	19 Nappy, 7 inch

Page Nine

Yellowstone shape from an old Homer Laughlin catalog.

Yellowstone shape, Buttercup decoration number Y2. A.D. cup and saucer
$15-18
covered sugar $10-12

Yellowstone shape covered casserole, Old Colonial/Gold Band
decoration number Y14. $30-35

Yellowstone shape, Caledonia decoration number Y94. plate $8-10
cup and saucer $8-10

Yellowstone shape plates. Left to right Old Colonial/Gold Band decoration
number Y14, Autumn Ivory decoration number Y80. $8-10

Yellowstone shape plate, Fruit Decorated decoration number
Y31 for Sears Roebuck. $8-10;

Yellowstone shape plate, Prairie Rose decoration.
$8-10

Yellowstone shape cream, Maxicana
decoration. $18-20

Yellowstone shape covered casserole, Raymond decoration. $30-35

Yellowstone shape saucers. Left to right, Wild Rose vellum glaze
decoration, Wild Rose ivory decoration number. $4-5 each

Yellowstone shape plate, decoration number Y15. $8-10

Yellowstone shape small plate, decoration number W132. There are variations in this pattern. $6-8

Yellowstone shape handled bowl and lid, decoration number Y43. $20-25

Yellowstone shape platter, decoration number Y137. $14-18

Yellowstone shape cake plate, decoration number CC19. $15-20

Yellowstone shape plate, decoration number Y232. $8-10

Yellowstone shape saucer, decoration number MS41. $4-5

Yellowstone shape plate, decoration number C-A-C-84. $8-10

Yellowstone shape plate, decoration number W132. There are variations in the decorations of W132. $8-10

Bibliography

Cunningham, Jo, *Homer Laughlin China-1940s & 1950s*, Schiffer Publishing, Atglen, Pennsylvania, 2000

Gates, William C. Jr., and Dana E. Ormerod. *The East Liverpool Ohio Pottery District Identification of Manufacturers and Marks*. Published by Society for Historical Archaeology, 1982.

Huxford, Bob and Sharon. *The Collector's Encyclopedia of Fiesta ®*, Eighth Edition, Schroeder Publishing. Collector Books. Paducah, Kentucky. 1998

Jasper, Joanne, T*he Collector's Encyclopedia of Homer Laughlin China*, Schroeder Publishing. Collector Books. Paducah, Kentucky , 1993.

Jervis, W. P. and J. F. O'Gorman Publishing Company, 1911. *A Dictionary of Pottery Terms*. O'Gorman Publishing, 1917

Lehner, Lois. *Lehner's Encyclopedia of U.S. Marks on Pottery, Porcelain and Clay*. Schroeder Publishing. Collector Books. Paducah, Kentucky, 1988

The Homer Laughlin China Collectors Association, *Fiesta®, Harlequin and Kitchen Kraft Dinnerwares* , Schiffer Publishing, Atglen, Pennsylvania, 2000